God's Memory Stones

Personal Memories of Love Given by God

Barbara J. Cornelius

God's Memory Stones
Personal Memories of Love Given by God

ISBN 978-0-9992698-0-0

interior design Dekie Hicks

WꝒ
wheredepony
Rome, Georgia
United States of America

Acknowledgements

I am so grateful to my family and friends, who prayed for me, inspired me, encouraged me, and assisted me in recording the stories in this book about the Lord's memory stones. Our living God always knows who we need in our lives to help us find the steps which He has laid out before us.

My grandson, Brandon Wyatt, helped me with my meager computer skills, so I could transmit in written word what the Lord had given me to share about Him. This young man is my treasure, as are all of my grandchildren.

My precious granddaughter, Alyssa Wyatt, who is pictured on the cover, always responds when I need her inspiration to go forward with what the Lord has laid on my heart. She makes my heart smile.

My grandchildren: Jeffrey, Martha, Abigail, Robert, Jacie, and Benjamin are also the joy and light of my world. My Heavenly Father knew how much I would be blessed by having them in my life. I love being their grandmother!

I was thrilled the days my son, Jeff Cornelius, and daughter Jennifer Snipes, were born, and I am still blessed every day of my life to be their mother. My son-in-law, Earl, and daughter-in-law, Julie, are truly the children of my heart. I will never stop being thankful to the Lord for His giving them to our family.

My husband, Larry, is absolutely the love of my life, and I am so grateful to God for His giving him to me to be my husband for all of these years. He is a wonderful, caring man who walks with the Lord and has a song in his heart. His gorgeous singing voice is truly a miracle, and I will always cherish how God touched him, so he could share his talent with so many people.

No one thrills me more, gives me more joy, and excites me more about the present and the future than my Lord Jesus. I pray that all the words in this book give Him honor and glory and tell others how awesome He is. Praise Him!

Table of Contents

Introduction

Isaiah 26: 8
O LORD, we have waited for You; The desire of our soul is for Your name and for the remembrance of You.

God's Word is so exciting! In chapters three and four of Joshua in the Old Testament, we read about the history of Israel passing through Jordon into the enemy territory of Canaan. When the Israelites marched into this enemy territory, God orchestrated a miracle that enabled them to travel across the Jordan River. These men of war in God's chosen nation came with their wives, children, families, cattle, tents, and all their personal effects. To make the situation even more dramatic, the crossing took place in the spring when the Jordan River was at flood stage and was overflowing its banks.

God purposely chose the time when the river was at its highest to demonstrate His power in parting the waters, so that the entire nation could cross on dry ground. After Joshua gave the order, they marched up to the river's edge, and then the Almighty power of God took over. When the priests, who were carrying the sacred Ark of the Covenant, first put their feet in the water's edge, the flow of water stopped. It not only stopped, it dramatically piled up in a heap, and the river went dry all the way down to the Arabah Sea. The Israelites then all crossed safely. With divine direction every step of the way, they crossed safely into Canaan.

Wow! What a sight that must have been! Would Israel always remember this dramatic event? God made sure. He spoke to Joshua and told him to build a memorial using twelve stones taken from the river. He was to use twelve men, one from each tribe so that all the people were represented. They were to also build this in the sight of the people at the place where they had their headquarters. God wanted them to see this as they rested that night. Not only that, He told Joshua to have the men take twelve more stones and set them up in the midst of the Jordan. These were to be piled up so high in a heap that the top might be seen above the water when it was clear or when the river was low.

The two sets of twelve stones were to be a constant re-minder of God's miracle for the Israelites when they crossed the Jordan River. This memory would be preserved when their children saw the stones, heard the story, and learned about the character of God. In the future, when *their* children asked what the stones meant, they were to pass the memory to them and tell them what God had done. These stones were memory stones for all of the generations of Israel. Today, when we read about them in God's word, they also become our memory stones.

God is continually creating miracles in our lives and asking us to remember what He has done. In *Genesis 28:10-18* we read about how Jacob responded when he had an encounter with the living God during a dream. In this Scripture we see Jacob having a supernatural experience that has since been shared by God's people for over three thousand years! Jacob saw a stairwell to heaven which was lined with angels, and heard God give him a personal message about the blessings that awaited him. Jacob decided to commemorate his personal encounter with God by taking the stone he had rested his head on during the dream and making it a memorial pillar. He then anointed this stone with oil and named it Bethel which means "house of God."

How does someone rest their head upon a stone? Jacob certainly did, and in so doing, his "pillow" became his memory stone. I have had my own experience with a stone that became a pillow. Over eleven years ago, my daughter Jennifer was in the intensive care unit at our local hospital, and her life hung in the balance. I could not leave her, and the only sofa and chairs in the intensive care waiting area were occupied. I took three small stone tables and pushed them together. I wearily lay down upon them, and then I prayed continuously during the night. The next morning, everything had changed. Jennifer had walked through the valley of death and emerged victoriously with God at her side. Those three stone tables became my memory stones. Now that I have told you about them, they can also be yours. God is so thrilling, and He is still doing for us what He did for His people throughout the Bible!

We have traditions, special dates and special places to help our children learn about God's work in our lives, but what about the memory stones He personally gives to us? Do we notice them? Do we tell others about them? He provides them throughout our lives. He wants us to not only remember them ourselves, but to also tell our children about what He has done for us. Then they become their memory stones to pass on to the next generation.

What makes up these personal memory stones? They come through people God places in our lives, mementos we receive during seasons in our lives, unexpected encounters with others, answered prayers, and even through brokenness that God touches with His healing hands.

It is my prayer that as you come and sit in my *stream of memory stones* which are described throughout this book, they will remind you of those God has given you. Recognize them. Enjoy them. Share them with others for the glory of our living God. He is so AWESOME!

Look at all the memory stones in the picture.
Are you reaching for yours? Are you sharing them?

Philippians 4:13

For I can do everything through Christ, who gives me strength.

Isaiah 42:15-16**

I'll take the hand of those who don't know the way, who can't see where they are going. I'll be a personal guide to them through unknown country. I'll be right there to show them what roads to take, make sure they don't fall in the ditch.

**The Message

Psalm 37:23

The LORD directs the steps of the Godly. He delights in every detail of their lives.

Chapter One

Memory Stones in a Study

A dream is fulfilled by the Hand of God

he retired pilot's helmet, worn when he flew an F-16 fighter jet, rested on a shelf in his study in the midst of several family photographs. It sat next to another helmet he wore when he flew an F-4 fighter jet. The two helmets were joined by other sentimental reminders of how the Lord had blessed his life. Models of vintage airplanes, plaques and framed photographs from milestones of flight school, a wood propeller from an antique airplane, a flag from his retirement from the Air National Guard and a flag from when he flew in combat missions over foreign soil years earlier were joined by a flag that had rested on his father's casket during his funeral twelve years earlier.

All of these mementos belonged to my cousin Rick who recently retired as a captain for a commercial airline company. I stood with him and admired all that he had placed in this space.

As a strong Christian man who recognizes the real treasures of life, he remarked to me, "All of this is just stuff!" I smiled at him as I responded, "No, what you see are your memory stones!"

My words sprang from a forty year old recollection of the time when Rick had shared with me his dream to become a pilot. He had recently unsuccessfully applied to flight school in the Air National Guard. He had only one more opportunity to apply before time ran out due to the age requirement. I remember his words from that long-ago time as if they had just been spoken, "Please pray for me to be accepted to flight school. Time is running out!" I agreed to support him in prayer, and now I was savoring the sight of a room full of "memory stones" the Lord had provided to remind both of us of what He had done when He answered that prayer.

My cousin's entire life has been a miracle for our family. My brother Bobby passed away one month before his tenth birthday, and our family fell into a long season of deep grief for a life lost before it really began. My Aunt Bette and my Uncle Babe, who was my father's younger brother, had been married for ten years and had not been able to have children. They had treated my brother, younger sister, and me as their own children. They spoiled us in all the ways children relish with love, books, and toys.

In the midst of our family's tremendous grief of losing my brother, Aunt Bette and Uncle Babe shared the news of an expected baby. God had set His plan in motion a month before Bobby died. He reached down to an aching family to bring comfort through the life of this baby. My cousin was born eight months after my brother died. We would not see Bobby arrive to adulthood and live a long life, but we would all savor the milestones of this male child.

I was only eight years old when my cousin Rick was born, but my memories are very vivid from that time because they were framed by great joy arriving in the midst of tremendous sorrow. My mother was a registered nurse and worked on the maternity floor of the local hospital. With God's perfect timing, she was able to be there with my aunt when she delivered her baby. Mother called home to tell my father about the birth. This was a time before sonograms, so parents had to wait until their child was born to know the sex. I can still hear the excitement in my father's voice when he repeated what she had shared, "It's a boy!"

The family that had lost its only son could now rejoice in the birth of a male child who had been born to the brother and sister-in-law who had had no children. A few years later my cousin Rick was joined by a brother and sister. God sent three children to my aunt and uncle after the loss of Bobby. Our families, who had always been close, became even closer as the children of both families "believed" they had two sets of parents who loved them unconditionally.

God has always had His hand on Rick's life, and our entire family has rejoiced with him each time he found the Lord's footprints leading from the present into the future. Rick has been on a long journey of faith to become what the Lord had inspired him to become and to give testimony of His faithfulness.

After Rick graduated from high school he was hired to work at Allison's Gas Turbine Company in Indianapolis, Indiana where his father had worked for almost twenty years. Although it provided an income for Rick and his new wife, he was not where his yearnings wanted to take him. He joined the Air National Guard and discovered his summer vacation service was giving him a glimpse of a different path for his life's work.

Soon after taking his first plane rides as a teenager, he had begun to dream about someday becoming a pilot. However, he felt this desire was an improbable journey for him. No one in the family on either side had ever received a pilot's license, and the expense and required education seemed insurmountable.

Yet, God was planting the seeds of desire in Rick's heart, long before the journey of realization began. God likes to do that for us, and then He encourages us to trust Him until we can see the path He is placing in front of us.

After Rick joined the Air National Guard, his job operating heavy equipment at the airport allowed him to see fighter jets landing and taking off. Observing this made his dream become stronger and more vivid. He knew he had a calling but not the knowledge of how he would be able to successfully arrive at that place in his future. That is where faith arrived to safely guide him to his heart's desire!

With full support from his wife Marcia, Rick left the security of his employment to become a college student. He loved sports in high school, but had been an average student in his academic classes. He simply had not been motivated to spend the time required to succeed in that area. God provided him with the partner he needed to urge him on and provide the confidence he needed for this huge leap in faith. Marcia echoed the words of *Philippians 4:13* when she responded to his dream to be a pilot, "Sure! You can do it! I am all for it!"

Rick's uncle, my father who taught high school business and government classes, had the credentials and the motivation to provide Rick with the assistance he needed with some of his classes. He spent many hours with him to make sure he succeeded. God had given him a burning need to do that for Rick, and it gave him great joy to be able to do it. God provided all that was required for Rick's path to success to be realized. God loves to do that for all of us who look to Him!

After Rick began taking private flying lessons from a pilot in the Air National Guard, he gained another mentor to support him in the pursuit of his dream. God surrounded Rick with those he needed for affirmation, so he could ignore the negativity some people offered him. Their discouraging words took a back-row seat to the cheering section God planted behind him.

God gave him "eagle's wings" and he finished a four-year college plan in two and a half years, meeting all the qualifications required to apply to flight school. Although others close to the selection process informed him that he had no chance, Rick was accepted. He had originally been fourth on the list with only one to be chosen. Circumstances beyond what anyone would have expected caused the other three to be disqualified. God paved a way that no one could have anticipated. Only someone secure in knowing God's will for his life could have had the courage to pursue this path.

The other students in his class had extremely impressive credentials and laughed good naturedly when he introduced himself, "I am just a dumb guy from the Guard!" The physical rigor of the training and endurance exercises in flight school served to test Rick's mantle of character and cement his desire to persevere.

Despite what could be recognized on paper about his classmates' superiority, he graduated in the top ten in his class. The favor of the Lord continued to be upon him as he walked in faith.

God's hand continued to guide Rick's life story as he became a fighter pilot flying combat missions over foreign lands and then afterwards, when he began his long career as a captain for a commercial airline company. A closet in his home houses two memory stones—his Air National Guard uniform and his commercial pilot uniform. They remind him of how God blessed his life and continues to give him favor beyond his expectations.

God added another chapter to this story about a year before Rick retired. He called me with the news that he had two free tickets for my husband and me to fly from the Atlanta airport which was near our home in Athens, Georgia to Washington D.C. with him as the pilot. I would never have dreamed over forty years ago, when Rick asked me to support him in prayer with his quest to become a pilot, the Lord would also give me such a magnificent memory stone of His love to share with my own family. When I sat on the plane and heard Rick as the captain giving routine announcements, I reveled in silent praise of my God! My Heavenly Father knew that this was my heart's desire and He granted it. Thank you Father! You delight my soul!

God blessed Rick with a wife who was synchronized in her heart with what He had written on Rick's heart, and with people He had appointed to support him every step of his journey. God also blessed him and Marcia with a son, Blake, and a daughter, Megan, to witness and remember what blessed lives from the Lord can mean to others. Blake has also become a pilot and Megan, who has a very successful career, married a man whose name is Bobby. God smiled on our family again when He gave us Bobby as a member of our family. My brother Bobby would have loved having another Bobby in the family.

The treasures in Rick's study which bring back wonderful memories can be destroyed and in time will cease to exist, but what is spoken and experienced in the name of the Lord about these keepsakes will carry on to future generations. I watch with joy as God directs Rick and Marcia's steps during this new phase of their lives as they discover all the new and exciting paths He has prepared for them. May every generation of their family and our entire family give praise, honor, and glory to our Lord.

When we study and read God's Word we can see how throughout time, our God has asked His people to remember what He has done in their lives and share these memories with others. When we share testimony of how the Lord resonates in our lives with our families, friends, and others we meet, we continue to plant memory stones that will never disappear.

Who do you need to share your memory stones with today? Do not leave this earth without sharing them, for they will live in the lives of others long after you have gone home to be with the Lord. Keep telling how God's story has unfolded in your life and give Him the glory He so deserves! He is so exciting!

Rick and I on a joyful day!

After receiving his pilot wings, Rick trained to
fly the F-4.

Rick and Marcia Spencer

"Two Hearts Syn-chronized"

Rick's Study

Share your memory stones for God's glory!

Psalm 145:1-4*

I lift you high in praise, my God, O my King! And I'll bless your name into eternity. I'll bless you every day, and keep it up from now to eternity. GOD is magnificent; he can never be praised enough. There are no boundaries to his greatness. Generation after generation stands in awe of your work; each one tells stories of your mighty acts.

*The Message

Isaiah 41:4

Who has done such mighty deeds, directing the affairs of the human race as each new generation marches by? It is I, the LORD, the First and the Last. I alone am he.

Chapter Two

Words from the Past that Nourish the Future

Memory stones can be made from words of encouragement

Darling! What a precious letter! I particularly enjoy letters that say something worth remembering! I, too, am happy to be your grandmother's sister. You delight my soul! His will—nothing more, nothing less, and nothing else! I think God has His hand on you, dear. After graduation, teaching, no common, ordinary teacher—a superior one. I would not have missed my experience as a teacher!"

These words were written to me long ago by my Great Aunt Nora in response to a letter I had written her. I recently rediscovered the letter in a scrapbook from my high school graduation of over fifty years ago. Her encouraging words about my choosing teaching as a life-long career were a prophecy of hope for my life. They helped nourish my conviction that I had heard God's voice about my future.

I retired ten years ago after a long teaching career. I loved being a teacher. I did not love every day, but I loved and felt blessed by each of my thirty-seven years! Aunt Nora's words mattered to me. They still matter to me today, because I believe they came from someone the Lord purposely placed in my life to steer me towards the future He had waiting for me.

My Great Aunt Nora was a wonderful, loving role model for our family, blessing everyone around her. When she was only about twenty years old, she married a man much older. His wife had died at a very young age and left him with three small children. Although she and her husband never had children together, she loved his children and raised them as her own. When they had been married about twenty years, he died and she remained a widow the remainder of her life.

Aunt Nora was definitely a "people person." She showered affection on her family which included nieces, nephews, and their children. Every generation that came along was adopted into her "circle of love." She adored and worshipped the Lord with her whole heart and this spilled out on others. All of her conversations and interactions with people, even strangers, were lively and full of joy. She remained forever young.

A couple of years ago, an unexpected package came in the mail from my sister, and I opened it to discover a book of poetry Great Aunt Nora had written over sixty years ago. Many years prior to her death, she had a collection of her work put in a booklet and had given copies to her nieces, nephews, and other family members. Now, Mother's copy had come to me.

One day I turned to one of her poems about the humor to be found in celebrating a seventieth birthday. I was reading it for the first time after celebrating my seventieth birthday a few months prior. In the "equality" of God's timing, my Great Aunt Nora and I were now the same age, and I could enjoy being seventy with her. I could not escape realizing the Lord's sense of humor and timing in giving me that supernatural moment. He is extremely creative in making those novel times happen for us and He knew it would be great fun for me to have that experience! I like to call these gifts from Him, "God Moments!"

I have continued to read the poetry written in this "memory stone" book and marveled that I am an eye witness to the faith walk my great aunt experienced all those many years ago. I feel her presence as I read about the emotions of joy, anxiety, fear and surprise she shared in her written work. She is still with me because of the words she recorded.

I keep Aunt Nora's letter and poetry in a special place—my prayer room. Almost thirty years ago when our home was being built as a spec house, the builder decided to take some of the attic space and build a large walk-in closet. It is an unusual closet because, half way up, three of the walls slant at a steep angle toward the ceiling. For many years, we used this space mainly for storage. Now, I can see it was another planned gift from the Lord. He knew that someday it would be my special place to meet with him. Although I can have my time with the Lord anywhere, I enjoy this particular area enormously. My grandchildren saw the wonderful Christian movie "War Room" a few years ago which was about a devoted Christian's prayer closet, and so they like to refer to my prayer room as my "war room."

In this room rests the antique secretary-desk where Great Aunt Nora sat when she penned her letter to me and perhaps wrote her poetry. This beautiful dark mahogany desk with small storage drawers and ornate locks and doors has resided in the homes of four women who loved the Lord. My Grandmother Overstreet inherited it from her sister, my Great Aunt. Grandmother Overstreet then gave the desk to my mother. It resided in Mother's home for over thirty years before she decided to down-size her living space and belongings before moving in with my sister. She entrusted this treasured piece of furniture to me for safe keeping, because she knew I recognized the sentimental value it had for our family. Mother has now been gone for a few years, and I savor the memories I have of its being in her home.

Someday, if it is in God's planning, this desk that holds so many memories will go to another family member. Even if this piece of furniture is somehow destroyed or lost, the memories about it will survive. It is soaked in prayer, and when I sit with my grandchildren in my prayer room, I share the stories of faith that came from the previous owners. God just loves to hear us do that kind of sharing with our families. His Word is baked with stories of Him telling us to remember His deeds and pass this sacred knowledge to other generations. He smiles on us when we are obedient to this! I love the thought of God smiling because I have done something to please Him! I frequently tell my grandchildren to make God smile in heaven!

I loved and adored my Great Aunt Nora! She died at the age of ninety-one, but she never grew old in spirit. God knew I needed to rediscover her letter and poetry and savor them in this season of my life. God lavishly weaves these connections of love in our lives. He does this for me all the time. He does that for you too!

There are two plaques on my desk. One reads "Only speak words that make souls stronger" and the other reads "words are so powerful they should only be used to bless, to heal, and to prosper." Great Aunt Nora did an amazing job of living this philosophy and she was generous with her words of exhortation. It was one of her spiritual gifts. Thank you, Aunt Nora for the deposit of joy you dropped into my spirit with your words. It is still there!

In the age of technology where we communicate primarily with email, facebook, texting, snapchat, and other ways, we find very few people practicing the habit of handwritten notes and letters. Some of the beautiful things they say to others will be forever forgotten, never having the chance to be savored many years after they are gone.

Your words matter. Share them in a way that will nourish others as our Lord has nourished you. Consider taking time to occasionally use "snail mail" and give someone you love a memory stone that can be anointed by the Lord to bless their lives! Who do you need to make smile today as they go to their mailbox and retrieve the contents? Maybe, by doing this you can even bless someone, long after you have left this earth, like my Great Aunt Nora did for me.

On Being Seventy

Between thirty and forty
I was distracted;
Between forty and fifty
I was ill at ease;
But from fifty to sixty
I was free from ills,
Calm and still my heart rejoiced,
Done with all profit
Nor did I still think of fame;
Yet far from illness,
And far from decrepitude, I have strength of limb
To go to see a new world—
To find new horizons.
When asked to write a poem,
I write a volume;
Nor do I complain too much
For I have arrived
At my allotted portion—Three score years and ten.

By **Nora Reed Smith**

Aunt Nora's Writing Desk

Send someone a note or card today and use your words to make them smile! God will smile too!

Genesis 22:1-2,9-12

Sometime later, God tested Abraham's faith. "Abraham!" God called. "Yes," he replied. "Here I am." "Take your son, your only son—yes, Isaac, whom you love so much—and go to the land of Moriah. Go and sacrifice him as a burnt offering on one of the mountains, which I will show you."

When they arrived at the place where God had told him to go, Abraham built an altar and arranged the wood on it. Then he tied his son, Isaac, and laid him on the altar on top of the wood. And Abraham picked up the knife to kill his son as a sacrifice. At that moment the angel of the Lord called to him from heaven, "Abraham! Abraham!" "Yes," Abraham replied. "Here I am!"

"Don't lay a hand on the boy!" the angel said. "Do not hurt him in any way, for now I know that you truly fear God. You have not withheld from me even your son, your only son."

Chapter Three

A Grandmother's Painted Memory Stone

Some of our memory stones are waiting to be claimed

The painting hung in my home for many years before I valued the message embedded on the canvas many, many years ago by my maternal grandmother. I remember how proud she was when she gave it to me, and how at the time I vaguely recognized the testimony she had lovingly portrayed with the brush strokes of her artist hands. The painting portrays Abraham and Isaac as they go up a mountain for the sacrifice of Isaac which God had asked Abraham to make.

Grandmother Overstreet's painting reflected her great faith. She loved going to church, loved reading her Bible, and loved the Lord. I still remember visiting her home as a young child and seeing her open Bible with her large magnifying glass placed on top of the page she had just read. Today, I have to smile when I see my magnifying glass on top of my Bible! I am grateful that large print Bibles are easily purchased in the

Christian bookstore nearby. I have placed one on my wish list for my next birthday!

When Grandmother's Bible was passed on to my Mother, it was not in pristine condition. It had obviously experienced a great deal of use. I feel so gratified seeing Grandmother's Bible like that. I absolutely love holding Bibles like hers in my hands-ones that have been worn out with love.

The leather cover of her Bible had multiple cracks and was no longer a solid black, and the pages inside revealed the wear and tear of hands that had touched them thousands of times. Her Bible was soaked with the prayers she offered up to her Heavenly Father through many tears and many moments of celebration. Her lifetime of knowing the Lord through studying His Word was reflected in so much of what she said and did with her family.

Grandmother had six children and lived on very little income. She planted a garden, did canning every season, made everything last that could be replenished or repaired, and spent frugally her entire life. When her husband, my grandfather, died he left her a small pension from the railroad company for which he had worked.

Even with her financial limitations, she always found a way to meet all of her monetary needs, and she even loaned money to her adult children when they needed it. My parents were blessed by this generosity after my nine-year-old brother died, and they had huge medical bills to pay. When it came time for them to repay grandmother, she told them she was cancelling their debt because she was gifting the same amount to her other children. She was a wonderful financial planner long before that became a career for many adults today! I am sure that all she did made the Lord proud of her! It makes me proud of her all over again, just to write these words.

Her creativeness was expressed in not only her paintings, but also her cooking, and her sewing. When my favorite cousin, Mary Dell, who was just a year older than me, and I spent the night with her, we not only had the treat of sleeping on her wonderful feather bed, we also occasionally had tremendous fun making cookies. After baking those sugar cookies and decorating them, they probably weighed a pound a piece! She may have had more than twenty grandchildren, but we were sure she loved us the best! We had the cookies to prove it!

She certainly always made Mary Dell and me feel special. I remember when we were around seven and eight years old, she made us matching gold corduroy dresses. She then decided we needed purses to complete our outfits. She took two round oatmeal boxes and cut them in half. She then covered them in the same fabric with a drawstring at the top for opening and closing. I always enjoyed a new outfit, even at my young age, and having one that matched my cousin's was definitely "the icing on the cake!" I was one happy grandchild!

Grandmother could whip up outfits rather quickly, because she had had a lot of practice making all of the clothing for herself and her children when they were growing up. Of course, in that era, most women could sew and routinely collected fabric and repurposed used clothing to keep their family clothed.

One of our family's favorite stories of Grandmother's sewing was about the wedding dress she made for my mother's sister who was two years older. When Grandmother made it, she intended for it to get double usage. Mother was engaged and was to marry my Father eight months after my aunt's wedding. What Grandmother did not know was that my parents had wed secretly a few months prior. Mother was in nursing training at the time and in the 1940's student nurses could not be married.

Mother had borrowed her sister's new blue wool suit and, unknown to her and the rest of the family, she used it for her wedding. She had no plans to wear the wedding gown sewn by Grandmother. Grandmother was pretty upset when Mother graduated and revealed she was already married. It's hard to know if Grandmother was the most upset about the secret marriage or that the wedding gown was only going to be worn once!

Somehow, the desire to sew was not passed on to my mother. She was great at mending torn clothing, but she didn't have any motivation to start from scratch. Perhaps, the "sewing gene" just skipped a generation. However, unlike my grandmother, I struggled with sewing. I simply didn't have the talent for it. In home economics classes, I had a lot of difficulty with even the simple projects we were assigned. One time I was making a simple skirt, but before I could finish it I cut a hole in it! My teacher was somehow motivated to give me a passing grade—I am sure it was out of pity!

Still, the desire to persist was passed on to me by my grandmother. I don't give up easily! I decided in my early twenties to teach myself to sew. In the 1960's sack dresses were popular, and I happily set out to make myself a new dress to wear to the elementary school where I was teaching. I will never forget the look on my principal's face when I wore it to school. I was so proud, but his face revealed he was not very appreciative of my handy work. Did I see the look of horror on his face? Not sure.

I obviously had not inherited my Grandmother Overstreet's skill in that department, but I happily continued with this hobby for many years. I even made outfits for my daughter when she was too young to stage a valiant protest. I have pictures of her in these "works of art" from when she was only a year old up to the age of nine. Some of them even had matching hats and purses. The inside of those dresses was a mess you would not want to see, but the outside was good enough for a pretty picture!

I remember looking at patterns that sometimes looked like "rocket science" to me and having to repeatedly tear out seams I had incorrectly sewn so I could redo them. I gave up sewing as a hobby many years ago, but in recent years I have realized that it taught me that adversity was not always my enemy.

Sometimes it is simply getting me to where the Lord wants me to be in life. The "redoing" is just part of the journey. Thank you, Grandmother Overstreet for inspiring me to sew and letting me see your perseverance in everything you did. I treasure the memory stone of seeing you do this in your faith walk with the Lord.

Today in my home, I not only have Grandmother Overstreet's painting, I also have a quilt she made for my father when he began his teaching career. Grandmother made individual squares and took yarn to embroidery the name of each student in his first class. This quilt, which must now be about eighty years old, spent many years in a cedar chest in my parent's house without my knowing what it was. Several years ago it found its way to my home, and to a closet with other things my mother had given me. Only recently did I realize what I had.

Finally recognizing what I had been given, I draped it over the back of a small love seat in my prayer room. As I have entered my "twilight years," I have become much more sentimental about these kinds of things as I remember my teaching career, watch my daughter in her twentieth year of being a teacher, and now see my oldest granddaughter go off to college to become a teacher. I value seeing where the thread of life is being woven through the generations by a loving heavenly Father.

Everything in my home that came from my grandmother's hands makes me remember how faith was entwined with all that she did. Her painting of Isaac and Abraham sits in the prayer room where I spend my quiet times with the Lord. Sometimes I take my grandchildren there for prayer and reading God's Word. I share with them the testimony given by their great, great Grandmother Overstreet. Grandmother is still teaching me and leading me by example, as I seek to give my own testimony for my Lord. Remembering her faith walk is a memory stone I cherish. I want to leave this same kind of memory for my family, because this is where they will inherit their greatest wealth.

Only recently did I fully understand the real value of my Grandmother's painting. It reveals a picture given to the world thousands of years ago when God pulled aside the curtain of time to give the world a look into the future. He was revealing what it would look like when He sacrificed His only Son for us! Isaac carrying the wood for the sacrifice on his back symbolizes Jesus carrying the wooden cross on his back. The lamb that comes out of the brush to rescue Isaac from being the sacrifice represents Jesus coming to save us. He came to rescue us from suffering the fate we deserve for our sins- eternal death and separation from Him!

When we look to Abraham, we have a glimmer of what it would be like for a father to sacrifice his son. Grandmother Overstreet knew what God had done for her, and she wanted her descendants to know it also. She wanted to leave this inheritance of spiritual wealth for all generations that followed her. The Holy Spirit guided her hands over the canvas as she painted God's story. Thank you, Father, for loving us that much!

Every generation gets caught up in its own problems, but God's plan embraces them throughout time. When your great-grandparents lived, God worked personally in their lives. When your great- great-grandchildren live, God will still work personally in their lives.

Grandmother Overstreet wanted all the generations who followed her to have a memory stone of God's love for their lives. I am passing mine on to my family. Now I pass it on to you. Pass it on to your family and tell everyone you know about Jesus!

Grandmother Overstreet on Larry's and My Wedding Day.
I love you still, Grandmother.

Examine God's Word closely. You will find memory stones to share with all generations of your family!

Isaiah 41:4 "Who has done such mighty deeds, directing the affairs of the human race as each new generation marches by? It is I, the LORD, the First and the Last. I alone am He."

Jeremiah 29:11-12

"For I know the plans I have for you," says the LORD. "They are plans for good and not for disaster, to give you a future and a hope."

Chapter Four

A Miracle Child Brought Home

Memory stones of love without boundaries

I sat in the narthex of our church and watched the beautiful little nine-year-old girl come bouncing through the door for Vacation Bible School. This child is a living memory stone for a few hundred people at our church, and watching her make her joyful entrance made me smile. She was meant to be in our midst and give us a blessing of redeeming hope in a world which constantly tries to steal our dreams. She is a vessel of joy for all of us!

When Elizabeth was born in China on March 2, 2007, she was placed in an orphanage with the distant hope that someone might come to adopt her. However, not just anyone was going to come for her. Even before she was born, God had a plan for her life which included Susan and Chris becoming her parents and raising her to know Him.

In the 1970s Diane Sawyer hosted a television show about the heart-breaking circumstances of children in orphanages in

China. At that time parents in China were permitted to have only one child, and "unwanted" children would often end up in orphanages. Susan, who was only twelve years old at the time, told her mother, "When I grow up, I am going to adopt a baby from an orphanage in China!" The Holy Spirit was even then whispering into her heart the plan God had to bless her life and the life of a baby girl.

As an adult, Susan developed medical problems which required surgery that eliminated her ability to have her own biological children. A few years after she and Chris married, they began their journey to become parents and earnestly researched adoption procedures. They then quickly decided to begin the process of adopting a child from China. God was directing their steps toward the future He had planned for them.

Susan and Chris began the long and tedious process to claim Elizabeth as their daughter a few years before she was born. They could see her in their hearts before she even began to rest in the womb of her biological mother. After the first round of filing the paperwork and paying all the fees, the legal process for adoption seemed to become a tangled mess. Then, dishearteningly, everything came to an abrupt halt. Sensitive deadlines had passed and passports, immigration papers, and other documents had to be redone. Chris and Susan had seemingly reached a dead-end street. If these parents wanted their baby, they would have to begin all over and re-file the required forms and also pay the expensive fees a second time.

This disheartened couple felt their dream of becoming parents was slipping through their fingers. They had been on this long journey for several years already and the "voice of reason" was beckoning, telling them that perhaps this was "not meant to be." However, our Heavenly Father is the master of navigating "dead end streets" and the path that had become entangled was simply designed to give God the glory for the steps that lay ahead.

Chris was greatly encouraged by dreams he had about his

daughter. He said, "I see a baby in a crib with other babies, and I know which baby is ours even though I can't see her face." Later, he shared with friends, "I can't stop trying to adopt her, because I see her in my arms!" All who were joined with Chris and Susan on this faith walk embraced Chris's visions of this child. These pictures from the future were a gift from the Holy Spirit. They gave Chris and Susan a hunger to persist on the long path that lay ahead.

On eleven different occasions, Chris and Susan traveled the one hundred and fifty miles round trip to the agency handling the adoption. They patiently and politely inquired on each visit about the process of the proceedings. Any message of discouragement was being drowned out by their prayers and those of everyone in their circle of loyal friends and relatives. The Lord was being magnified as the Holy Spirit was at work directing a victorious outcome.

Finally, the long-hoped for news came that their daughter was waiting for them in China. All the hurdles placed in their path had been taken care of by the One they had entrusted with their dream- the living God!

One additional burden for Susan was that she had never flown before. However, the timing of the very first flight of her life, which would take her all the way to Beijing, China, was a part of God's perfect plan for her and Chris. She took medication with her to the airport to assist with the nervousness she anticipated would happen during the long fifteen-hour flight. Susan, however, never felt the need to take anything for her nerves, even though there was significant turbulence during part of the flight. She experienced supernatural calm the entire time. God had prepared for every detail of this miraculous journey and Susan experiencing this milestone was given a "postmark" of His divine power. He gave her this peace to show her and others that He was on the job!

Susan and Chris arrived in Beijing excited and anxious to see their baby, only to discover that the Chinese thought they should spend four days sight-seeing. They had been patient for so long, and now they had to practice this gift of the spirit for a little longer. Finally, on the fifth day, as they anxiously waited with other parents for their adopted babies, ten-month-old Elizabeth was brought to them. They could finally hold their baby daughter!

As requested by the orphanage, a few months before this first meeting, Chris and Susan sent their baby daughter a care package with several items and they decided to also include a bear with a recording of their voices: "This is Chris, your daddy. This is Susan your Mommy. We are coming to get you!" Their hope was that sending this would give their baby familiarity with their voices and make her more comfortable with them when they met.

When the other babies were given to their new parents, they cried with the pain of separation of leaving the only caring arms they had known. However, Elizabeth did not cry or show any signs of being uncomfortable. Interestingly, she had not received the bear introducing her parents' voices to her. Yet, she rested comfortably and peacefully in their arms. The Holy Spirit was at work insuring her that she was finally home in the arms of her parents.

After fourteen busy and stressful days in China, the new family flew home. Chris and Elizabeth had flown into China on the heels of the country's worst snowstorm in sixteen years, and on their return trip home they were delayed at one point by another historic storm. Yet, God smoothed out all the rough places of their journey so they could share with others their story of His faithfulness to them!

Back home twelve family members greeted them at the airport. Many pictures were taken to record the abundant joy of these new parents. One of the most treasured ones showed Chris standing alone with Elizabeth in his arms. The picture of his future daughter he had seen in his spirit had come to fruition, and was now one that could be captured by a camera for everyone to see. The baby bed in Chris and Susan's home which had sat empty for three years was about to be filled. God did that.

Still, God was not through with the miracle story of Elizabeth coming home. He did something totally unexpected and inconceivable in order to bring another blessing to the family. Chris's mother had been tenderly and totally engaged with the quest of bringing this child into the family. Although at the age of seventy-six she suffered from multiple and very serious medical problems, the dream of someday seeing her granddaughter gave her new optimism for the future. She desperately wanted to see a picture of this long-wanted baby, and had even expressed a fervent desire to accompany Chris and Susan when they flew to China to bring her home. God had given her a deep penetrating love for a grandchild she had yet to meet. Sadly, this expectant grandmother died in 2007 a few months before the trip to China took place, and the picture she ached for never reached her hands. It arrived two months after her death, and Elizabeth came home a few months after that.

Yet, God was not through. He had thrilled so many hearts with His answer to prayers for this child and grandchild. He now gave the family another way to experience the supernatural reach of His love.

Almost two years later the family, living in a home which had once been the home of Elizabeth's deceased grandmother, experienced another sign from God about the enormous reach of His love. Elizabeth, now almost three years old, awoke from a nap with a surprising story! She had become a very talkative toddler and had sweet, animated conversations with her parents. She excitedly told them, "Nanny came and visited with me. She told me that she is my grandmother, and she helped me sing my ABC's!" Chris's mother had been called "Nanny" by all of her grandchildren, but Elizabeth had not known this.

Her parents at first thought she had had a sweet dream about her only living grandmother. Elizabeth, who called Susan's mother "Gigi", when asked if it was her, said, "No, that was not who came to see me!" Pressed to identify the lady who had come to her, Elizabeth shared enough details to stun them with the belief she was talking about the grandmother who had died a year before she had come to the United States.

Elizabeth described her grandmother as wearing a pink dress and large glasses, and introducing herself as her "Nanny." Shown a picture of her deceased grandmother with her twelve brothers and sisters, Elizabeth, without any prompting, quickly identified her. She again told her parents how her grandmother in heaven had sung with her.

Elizabeth had never met this loving grandmother, but yet her spirit had received her love. How is this possible? Maybe we don't have to have all the answers on this side of eternity. Perhaps, we can just rejoice in the treasured words of a beloved child and know that God loves us and sometimes lets us experience His love through things we cannot explain. God never wastes anything in believers' lives. Somehow, He weaves everything they experience into the tapestry of their faith. Maybe He even does that for a Grandmother who longed to tell a grandchild she had never met, "I love you!"

Elizabeth has become a source of delight for everyone who meets her and has the privilege to watch her grow physically and spiritually. This miracle child placed by the Lord in a home of parents who love Him has become a blessing to an entire community.

She has received many words of love from all who have been blessed to participate in this miracle, and God even gave her an extraordinary communication of love that cannot be explained in human terms. These messages have gone into her spirit to confirm that she is a memory stone for many people's lives and a vital part of God's world. The knowledge of her role in God's kingdom is treasure that will remain in her spirit for the rest of her life.

Our assignment from our exciting God is to share His love with others, so they can experience the miracle of His presence here on earth and into eternity. God gives us living memory stones like Elizabeth, so that we can remember and recognize what He is doing daily in our lives. Who do you know in your life that does this for you? Are you being a memory stone for Him in someone's life? Remember! Share with others what you remember and let your story live past your time on earth. Give God the glory! Praise Him!

Chris holding Elizabeth in his arms. He first held her in his dreams!

Elizabeth and her family 2017

See why she makes all of us
smile! Thank you, Father!

creek photos
courtesy of Bryan
White,
Whitelake Studio

Psalm 111: 2-4

How amazing are the deeds of the LORD! All who delight in him should ponder them. Everything he does reveals his glory and majesty. His righteousness never fails. He causes us to remember his wonderful works. How gracious and merciful is our LORD!

1 Corinthians 15:43

Our bodies are buried in brokenness, but they will be raised in glory. They are buried in weakness, but they will be raised in strength.

Chapter Five

Butterflies

God gives us memory stones in nature

My attention was riveted on the vibrant, multi-colored butterfly as it kept circling me and occasionally landing on my arm and hand. I couldn't believe it was doing that. It was as if the butterfly wanted to get my attention! I knew it was not a coincidence. I felt this encounter was just for me, that I was receiving a message of love and encouragement from my Father. I thought to myself, "That is so like you!" I believe God is communicating to us like that every day. I love butterflies! He knows that.

I have a sofa in my study which is upholstered with a fabric of gold and rust butterflies on a dark brown background. The butterflies, which are all different sizes, appear in the midst of green ferns and gold flowers. My husband and I purchased this sofa for our living room almost forty years ago. Since we infrequently use this room, it received very little wear over the years.

Several years ago we moved this sofa into my study, and except for the faded bottom cushion, it's in fairly good condition. I recently gave some thought to finally replacing it with a new and perhaps more modern looking sofa, and so I browsed in the local furniture stores for something I would enjoy as much as my butterfly sofa. I came up empty handed, and instead bought a small comforter to cover the worn bottom cushion. I just couldn't give up my butterflies! They still make me smile.

I am not alone in appreciating butterflies. I have a good friend who has a large purse covered with butterflies, and I have told her that if it suddenly disappears, I know of several people, including myself, she might want to check out!

People all over the world are fascinated with butterflies. They collect pictures of them, purchase clothing with their images, buy ornamental objects in their likeness, and write inspirational messages about them. God knew how butterflies would bless mankind when He included them in His creation plan. He has embedded thousands of personal messages in nature in this way to communicate His love for us!

A recent widower in our town purchased butterfly decals to place on a large window of his house. His wife had been fascinated by butterflies, so seeing the decals on his window somehow made him feel closer to her. God knew we would be blessed with His message of hope when He created so many beautiful, living things on this earth. The butterfly is just one of them, and He knew that people like this grieving husband would find solace from them.

Over twenty years ago our church was devastated by the sudden death of our pastor's wife. Dolly Owens was only sixty-four when she headed to a grocery store, and, blinded by the late afternoon sun blocking her line of vision, pulled out in front of a large truck. She died instantly.

Our pastor Herb Owens and his wife had been spiritual equals and complemented each other in ways that blessed our entire church. Dolly was open and gregarious. During the few years she was with us, she gifted us with narratives of women in the Bible. When she would walk into our sanctuary during the worship service dressed as one of the characters from the Bible and speak to us, we were transported back in time thousands of years. She portrayed Mary, the mother of Jesus, the woman Jesus met at the well, Esther, and several others. Dolly's portrayals of these historical women from the Bible brought them from the past right into our lives today. We felt that not only were these women alive, but that we were also right there in their midst. Through her talent and love for the Lord, she made God's Word come alive for our congregation. She gave testimony of the Lord in all that she did while she was with us. We were so thankful for her.

Herb, who was less out going but greatly loved, preached from the pulpit with the heart of a man who knew and adored the Lord. He loved the old hymns and frequently at the conclusion of his sermons, felt inspired to sing one of them with his beautiful tenor voice. What a wonderful couple they were! Herb delighted in Dolly and she in him.

This amazing couple, who had four adult children, had been married thirty-nine years when Dolly pulled out in front of that truck and slipped into eternity. All of us in the church sought comfort for Herb and for ourselves. We craved a memory stone of God's consistent love in the midst of heartbreak.

A group in our church was inspired to consign a local artist to paint two cloth wall hangings three feet by ten feet. These were to hang in the narthex. The artist painted large majestic butterflies in glorious colors of blue, red, green and purple onto the fabric. Over the years these hangings have been in place, many individual and family pictures have been taken in front of them. People are just drawn to the butterflies. Dedicated to the memory of the beautiful, loving woman who had blessed our congregation, they have now hung there for twenty years. Every time people walk into the church foyer, the butterflies are there to greet them. Over and over, they glorify our God for what He lovingly gave to all of us.

We can appreciate what God has done when we revel in the artistry of metamorphosis that results in a butterfly. Today, we have the technology to gain a glimpse of God's unlimited power. We are so blessed to have modern DNA analysis and MRIs to reveal the amazing choreographed steps that take place during each stage of the transformation of the butterfly. God gave us these "ring side seats" so we can appreciate some of the thrilling events in nature that are surrounding us every day. God has a spectacular show awaiting us every day when we wake up. He is just waiting for us to notice these works from His hands!

Everyone loves God's story of His butterfly and how it begins with a caterpillar crawling on the earth, before building a chrysalis which becomes its home. At this stage of development, the caterpillar looks like it has been imprisoned and is no longer free to explore the earth. However, the constituent parts of the caterpillar are being devolved into a mysterious molecular soup. Leaving the chrysalis, it emerges as a being that is totally different. No longer able to move only by crawling, this new creature now has enormous freedom.

The butterfly now has wings that allow it to explore dimensions previously out of reach. Eyes that once distinguished only light from dark now experience dimensions of color and acuity. Once it merely existed to eat. Now, it indulges the nectar of a previously unimaginable new world. Wow! What once looked like a doomed existence inside a prison now turns into a thrilling journey.

God uses every butterfly to give us a memory stone of hope in the midst of the stinging heartache delivered when death removes those we love from our lives. He tells us to observe that the butterfly goes into a chrysalis (casket) only to emerge stunningly as a beautiful being that is not even close to what it was in its previous existence. He promises that this will be the story of our transformation after death.

God uses the butterfly to give us a preview of the experience we will have with our resurrected bodies. Because Jesus rose from the grave, we will rise again! When Jesus calls our names, we will not only be completely renewed and restored, we will be better than we ever were in our earthly bodies! We will be gloriously like our Savior! *1 John 3:2 says, "Beloved, we are God's children now, and what we will be has not yet appeared; but we know that when he appears we shall be like him, because we shall see him as he is."* Can you imagine anything more exhilarating to experience than to be like our Savior?

Who do you know that needs to hear this story about the butterfly? Who do you need to tell about the hope that God gives freely to us? Let it be a memory stone in your life and share it with others so they can cherish and possess this joy about eternal life!

Stop and ponder all of this the next time you marvel at the butterfly coming into your line of sight! Offer thanksgiving to God for all the love He lavishes on you and stop to worship Him for who He is! He is so awesome!

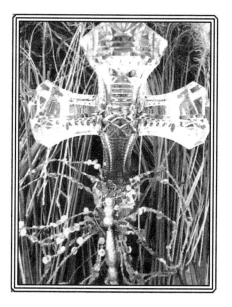

Don't miss the lesson of joy the butterfly brings to the world!
Worship the King and share His message of love and hope for all
people!

These are Dolly Owen's butterflies! In the midst of her absence, by the Hand of God, she is still blessing us!

A Psalm of David
Psalm 34:18-19

The LORD is close to the broken-hearted; he rescues those whose spirits are crushed. The righteous person faces many troubles, but the LORD comes to the rescue each time!

Revelation 21: 5

And the one sitting on the throne said, "Look, I am making everything new!"

Chapter Six

God's Memory Stones from Brokenness

He makes us new for His glory

The large ceramic frog's broken pieces were stored in a plastic bag in the back of a closet. Rambunctious children had knocked it off a table. With so many broken pieces, the frog looked beyond repair. Although the frog certainly qualified for the trash, its owner didn't have the heart to throw it away. Instead, Adam stored it in the back of his closet for over sixteen years.

The few times Adam discovered it again, he remembered his close childhood friend who had given it to him so many years ago. When Adam was five years old, this friend and her parents moved in next door. One day, feeling lonely, Adam decided to knock on their door and ask if they had any children. They introduced him to their daughter, Sheree, who was the same age. The parents and children all became the best of friends, and Adam and Sheree were inseparable for several years.

47

She and Adam loved to give each other gifts. When Sheree spotted the frog next to the sink in her mother's kitchen, she excitedly asked if she could give it to Adam. These two young playmates both loved frogs, and she just knew he would love this frog. He did. More than she could have imagined.

When Sheree and Adam were teenagers, she and her parents moved away, but Adam never forgot her. Adam kept his broken frog for all those years because he savored his past memories of a childhood friend. They brought joy to him.

Adam's wife shared the story of the broken frog with me, and we decided to see if it could be restored as a surprise Christmas gift for him. I have always been attracted to broken things and love the challenge of seeing if they can be repaired or repurposed. I have a hot glue gun that I use frequently (I will let you guess why that is necessary), and I do love the challenge of seeing what creative results can come from using it!

I once repaired a large ceramic vase (Yes, I broke it!) with my hot glue gun, and then I placed silk flowers over the cracks so no one could see it was once broken. It actually looked more attractive to me repaired than when it had been unblemished. I felt in that moment of observation that I was hearing the Lord whispering to me, "You once were broken, but now look at your beauty!" Remembering the transformation of my broken vase gave me the inspiration to see if I could repair the frog and produce similar results. I certainly embraced the opportunity to see what God had in mind for this broken frog!

I carefully placed all the pieces on a table to see how they might fit together. It was like assembling an intricate puzzle, but gradually I began to see the image of the frog materialize. I discovered my hot glue gun would not do a neat enough job this time, so I used super glue to reassemble it. (I thought about Jesus being my "superglue" as I did this.) I then concealed the places where the jagged pieces came together by gluing small ribbons and tiny silk flowers over them.

I rummaged in my kitchen cabinets and found a yellow ceramic dish I had purchased recently on impulse and decided to use it for the frog to sit on. Surprisingly, the dish was a perfect match, and the coincidence of that made me smile! To finish the project, I added two things to the dish- a small wooden cross and a copy of Scripture that celebrates God's miraculous power to bring restoration in the midst of brokenness. I could see that the Lord was using the story of the broken frog from Adam's past to give him a message of encouragement and hope for his future.

In today's troubled world, this message is sorely needed by all of us. Adam especially needed to hear it because several years previously, he had experienced a great tragedy. He had been riding home from a fishing trip with his best friend who was driving. They were involved in an accident . . . One moment there was laughter and joy. The next moment there was enormous pain and devastation. Several years later, Adam had healed from the physical trauma but the emotional suffering of losing someone he had loved so much remained. Adam needed continued blessings of hope and comfort to ease the pain of losing his best friend. The Lord is always faithful in providing these because He sees and feels our anguish.

Adam was thrilled when he opened the Christmas gift and saw his restored frog. He took the small wooden cross that had been placed next to the frog and hung it on a string in his car to remind him of the message he had been given.

Perhaps, the frog was meant to be broken and repaired so as to lend comfort at this particular point in his life. God, who can make all things new, has perfect timing. What is it about God's tender touch in the midst of brokenness that reveals His love in a way that nothing else in the universe is able to do? God takes our brokenness and restores us to a beauty that the world cannot always recognize. He reveals it in small moments like a ceramic frog being repaired as a sign of His presence, and He reveals it in huge moments where millions of people can observe and marvel. In this world broken things are despised and thrown out. Anything we no longer need, we throw away. Damaged goods are rejected and that includes people. The world is full of hurting people with broken hearts, broken spirits, broken relationships, and broken bodies.

The 2017 Memorial Day Concert in Washington D.C. gave testimony of God's healing power for the audience in attendance and for millions watching on television. Army Captain Luis Avila sang "God Bless America" while sandwiched between two very attractive women. All attention was drawn to him. You literally could not take your eyes off him, even though one of the women was a professional singer. It was his voice, somewhat off key, that soared and penetrated the hearts of everyone listening.

Captain Avila served three combat missions in Iraq before being sent to Afghanistan in 2011. Two days after Christmas, he was with five other men returning to base in an armored car when a six hundred pound IED exploded under them and cut their vehicle in half. Three of the men died in the explosion and Captain Avila was gravely injured. He was taken to a hospital in Germany where his survival seemed to be in great doubt.

He had suffered horrific injuries: the loss of his left leg, a traumatic brain injury, and a fractured spine which resulted in complete paralysis. In the midst of the unbelievable trauma, he experienced two strokes and two heart attacks. Later, he was transported to a hospital in Texas where he remained on life support and in a coma. His diagnosis for survival was very bleak. How could anyone survive under these conditions? God had an answer for that question.

When Avila's wife Claudia first saw him, she could barely recognize him through all the bandages on his body and all the life-saving machines attached to him. She was gently told by the medical people who cared for him, "Let him go." She and her family replied, "No." They did not believe that God's plan for his life was coming to an end. They believed they were supposed to fight courageously for their loved one's life.

Together, they fought as "warriors" for his regained consciousness by playing his favorite music: The Beach boys, The Beatles, and even Beethoven's "Ode to Joy" over and over. They spent hours talking to him, and most of all praying aloud asking his Heavenly Father to awaken him. They believed that not only could God hear their voices, but also somehow their loved one could hear every word, every song, and every prayer of faith.

Finally, Captain Avila, on the fortieth day, woke up to greet his family. He whispered through his trach tube, "What day?" Upon hearing the date, he said, "Taxes?" He had been injured a few weeks before their taxes were due and was asking if they had been paid. Oh my, did God's angels smile when they heard this conversation! He had spent forty days in his "desert", a coincidence of God's timing, and now he was coming back to his family!

Avila cried when he heard three of his buddies had died when the IED hit their vehicle. He wondered, "Why couldn't I have saved them?" There is no answer to that question on this side of heaven. But surely, when Avila goes home to the Lord, God will reveal the answer and his three friends will be waiting.

Obviously Avila had a life story that was not yet finished. Today, five years later and after seventy surgeries he is an out-patient at Walter Reed Hospital. He spends eight hours a day, five days a week there to receive physical therapy, occupational therapy, speech therapy, music therapy, and on-going medical treatment. He has been doing this for five years. He struggled for two years to be able to speak a full sentence. Yet, today he sings every day, plays his harmonica, and shares his faith.

He says, "Soldiers fight for what they believe in. Claudia and I pray every day to be able to meet that challenge. I want a new job which enables me to help encourage wounded vets." He and his wife say they do not see the physical disabilities. They see the possibilities. His three sons see the memory stone of their father's courage and say that his determination to live out his life for God's purpose has inspired them to be better people.

When Captain Avila sang "God Bless America" on national television he sang from his wheel chair. His music therapist stood next to him and sang with him as did a professional singer. This man of faith stunned the world with a message of hope about how God could use someone like him to show what victory over brokenness sometimes looks like in His kingdom. He sang from the top of his lungs and the countenance of the Lord adorned his face. All in attendance could see a great man of faith who had been transformed in his spirit for the glory of God. He became a memory stone of hope and inspiration for millions of people that day.

God continues in today's world of brokenness to give signs of His love and power by making us new. He does it with the restoration of those small things in our lives that carry great sentimental value like Adam's broken ceramic frog. He does it miraculously with the bodies and spirits of those who have suffered catastrophic injuries like that of Captain Avila. He can also do this for you, no matter where you are experiencing brokenness in your life.

To many people in the world, broken things are often despised as worthless, but God can take what has been broken and remake it into something spectacular. He can make any of us new. He can use our broken hearts, broken spirits, and even our broken bodies for His glory.

Our God does what the world says is impossible, and with the same power he used to create the universe, He restores us our minds, spirits, and souls. He allowed His own Son's body to be broken for us, so that we could be restored and renewed for life eternal. All we need to do is accept this gift. Give Him your brokenness and become new in Him.

Adam's Frog

Doesn't that make you smile? I am pretty sure it made God laugh!

† Barbara J. Cornelius †

Psalm 66:19

But God did listen;
He paid attention to my prayers.

Jeremiah 32: 26-27

Then this message came to Jeremiah from the LORD: "I am the LORD, the God of all the peoples of the world. Is anything too hard for me?"

Mark 11:24

"I tell you, you can pray for anything, and if you believe that you've received it, it will be yours."

56

Chapter Seven

Let Your Answered Prayers Be Memory Stones

God hears our voices when we speak to Him

She stood at the door of an unfamiliar house expecting to recognize absolutely no one in the Bible study that was being held inside. Being somewhat shy and frequently ill at ease in social situations, even with people she knew, this was unnerving! So why did she make this decision to be here?

This lady was me almost fifty years ago, but the memory of that day is still vivid. I had learned about the Bible study from someone whom I actually found very irritating at that time. My husband Larry was a graduate student in the College of Veterinary Medicine, and Namoi was the wife of my husband's older friend who was also a graduate student at the same university. She was twenty years older than I was and had obviously decided to take me on as her "project." She frequently brought Christian literature to my house, strongly suggesting it would bring a tremendous blessing if it were read. During one of her visits, she left a hand written invitation to a Bible study. For

57

some reason, I didn't throw it away like I did with all the other things she brought.

I can still recall on that particular morning all those years ago, picking up the invitation and realizing the study began that day. I also noticed it was conveniently located in my own neighborhood and would be held during the time my two-year-old son would be in nursery school.

I don't recall how I transitioned from absorbing that information to actually going to the study. I just went. That was totally not like me, because I always deliberated and planned ahead for any social events. I am not someone who frequently thrives with spontaneity. I once had a college roommate who joyfully and naturally did things on the spur of the moment, and although I loved being around her, her gift did not rub off on me!

Naomi had recognized that my husband and I were not attending church and experiencing much of a spiritual life. She had been determined to do something about that, but her efforts simply annoyed me. I tried to avoid her whenever possible. I had been raised in a Christian home and had gone to the same small church my entire life before leaving for college. I was now in a new and different season in my life. Somehow, after graduating from college and getting married, I drifted away from my Christian beliefs. They no longer defined who I was.

What had happened to my faith? My journey away from the Lord began with a comparative religion class I took my last year in college. I had misguidedly selected this elective course as a way of deepening my faith. I studied many different religions and their versions of how they saw our Creator and His relationship with people on earth. Billions of people around the world were confident of the truth as they found it in their individual religions, and their truth was not the same as mine. Learning all of this created seeds of doubt which began growing in my mind. I had never encountered anything like this when I was growing up and attending my very small Carbon

Methodist Church in Carbon, Indiana. I simply was not mature enough in my faith at that time to not be influenced by the curriculum of this class.

The Lord was watching all of this, and because He sees me and cares about all that I do, He had a plan. He always does. He let me see His miraculous power in two incidents He knew I would never forget. He was arming me for the spiritual battle that awaited me in the future.

The first one took place over a year after I graduated from college and married my husband. I was returning home that day from the school where I taught sixth grade, when suddenly the left rear wheel on my car flew off! I had been traveling over fifty miles per hour on a busy four lane highway. After skidding all over the road, the car left the road and headed for a deep ravine. I believed I was about to die. Suddenly, without slowing down, the car spun around and came to a stop at a right angle to the highway.

Unbelievably, none of the many cars and trucks on the road hit me. I was totally unharmed, and the only thing wrong with my car was a missing wheel. Two policemen arrived at the scene to assist me and were told by a passing truck driver, "She did an amazing job keeping the car on the road after it lost the wheel!" The policemen then searched the grassy area next to the highway and found the missing wheel. Surprisingly, they also located three of the four lug nuts that had held it in place. They kindly put the wheel back on the car, and then smiled as they told me, "Have a safe trip driving home!"

I didn't dare tell them what I was thinking, "Are you kidding me?" I meekly returned to my car. For many days, I kept saying to myself, "I should have died! How can I still be here?" I was certain that I must have had supernatural assistance to still be alive, but the complete realization of God's assistance to me during the accident was yet to be realized by me. Years later I came to believe God sent angels to help me that day.

A year after my accident the Lord gave me a second opportunity to see His hand on my life. We moved to Boston for my husband's small animal internship, and I began looking for another job. I knew we would not be able to make it financially if I did not have a teaching position. However, everywhere I applied they told me there were a few hundred people applying for the few positions they had. To make matters worse, I was only going to be there for one year, and felt I needed to share that information during interviews. Despite the doubts that were beginning to surface in my faith, the Lord gave me the unshakeable belief that I would be given a job.

Finally, a few weeks before the school year started, I found favor with the assistant superintendent of a small school system. He was one of the people who interviewed me, and I felt a special rapport with him. A few weeks later, I decided to call him and ask about the status of my application. Not only did he take my call, he told me they were waiting on one of my references to respond. Then he said something that still makes me smile when I remember it, "You know what, I am just going to offer you the job anyway!"

Mary Lee Burbank Elementary needed someone to fill in for a sixth grade teacher who was going on a one year sabbatical. Somehow the school system had decided I would be the perfect person to meet this need. Again, I believed I had experienced supernatural assistance. Years later I marveled at all the blessings I received with the gift of that teaching position.

Yet, a few years after these two miraculous events, my faith began to slowly disappear. The unanswered questions planted in my mind from my college class began to resurface and take root in my spirit. Worse, my husband and I were not motivated to locate a new church when we moved to Boston and then Columbia, Missouri. We did not worship anywhere. I now had nothing to counteract the seeds of doubt that had been planted.

I gradually lost my desire to read my Bible and seek out Christian friends. I did not pray at all. As far as I was concerned, God had just disappeared from my life. I no longer thought about those two miraculous incidents, and the memory of them blurred. I stopped giving God any of my time. All relationships need tending to or they will simply cease to exist. The one we have with our living God is especially vulnerable, because Satan is constantly seeking victory over us and is always pulling us in the opposite direction. The less time we spend with our Lord, the more successful Satan can be. For this period of my life, I did not recognize God in my life, and I did not tend to my relationship with Him.

The Lord saw my plight and gave me a third miracle. He sent Naomi into my life all those years ago. As a result of her persistence, without any advance planning on my part, I appeared at a Bible study with my Bible in hand. After I walked in and sat down, I met women who were strangers to me, but their friendliness drew me in and made me feel comfortable right away. God's spirit permeated the room. I learned they were studying the book of Genesis and discussing the characteristics of God. Someone read aloud a familiar verse: *Genesis 1:27 "So God created human beings in his own image. In the image of God he created them; male and female he created them."*

We began to discuss the meaning of this verse and identify the human characteristics we have because we were made in the image of God. Some of the ones we identified made us laugh. We gleefully decided that God must love laughter and He sometimes laughs with us. I know He was smiling that day over all that transpired as we pored over His Word, and I feel that we were most certainly feeling His pleasure on us.

God's Word is living. That means when receptive spirits read His Word, He breathes on them. Suddenly, in those first minutes of this Bible study God came back to life for me, and amazingly I felt great joy in being where I belonged. God's Spirit just washed over me. He had let me experience a time of being lost. I had walked away, but I discovered that He had not gone anywhere. He was still right beside me.

How was it possible that I arrived at a Bible study I never decided to attend? I learned later that before the study began, Naomi, after inviting me, sat with others and prayed fervently over the name of every person who had been invited. I believe I was prayed to that study, and I will never forget experiencing God in that way. Thank you, Naomi, for being so faithful to God's calling to search out His lost.

This experience became a huge memory stone for me about the amazing power of prayer. However, my new walk with the Lord was not one my husband appreciated. For years we argued about his infrequent church attendance. I knew he believed in God, but he just didn't always feel the need to join me and our children in worshipping at church. Instead, many Sundays he liked to play golf and participate in other activities. My prayers and those of others covered him for many years. Those prayers were answered after Larry and I had been married for over thirty years when he accepted the Lord as his Savior. I cried as I stood with him at the altar of our church and witnessed him being baptized and tearfully speak his profession of faith. God had lovingly placed both of us in His arms. We both were prayed back to God's fold by dedicated prayer warriors.

Another one of my friends from that Bible study all those years ago inspired me to be a prayer warrior and pray about everything. She convinced me that God cares about everything I do and every decision I make. She told me," If you just consult him about the big issues, you will not feel a need to talk to Him every day!" I have followed her advice the last forty years of my life. I am frequently delighted to see my Heavenly Father answer prayers for small matters which are not seen as being of great importance. I have also recognized many, many of His miracles which I might have missed, if I had not been blessed by His presence throughout my daily life.

Many times we offer up prayers and then seem to go on our merry way, forgetting to notice when God has answered those prayers. We frequently only notice the ones where we don't receive the answers we wanted. We know when we ask for a miracle and see it answered that God was surely at work. However, what about all the other times when we see simple requests granted? Do we recognize God for those answers?

We ask for safe traveling, for needs of our friends and families to be granted, for our food to be blessed, and even for the ability to bring good into the lives of others. We ask for these things all the time, and frequently fail to stop and give thanks to God for favorable answers. Instead, they escape our minds and fail to become our memory stones.

Let your answered prayers be memory stones that you share with family members, friends, and perhaps when God provides the opportunity- total strangers. Remember to tell Him thank you and praise Him for who He is! He not only listens every day to your voice- He is waiting for you to speak!

Psalm 77:11

But then I recall all you have done, O LORD; wonderful deeds of long ago.

Chapter Eight

Memory Stones from Unexpected Encounters

God gives us memory stones that surprise us

The eager female voice on our answering machine was one I had never heard before. It was obvious the person who spoke was very disappointed upon not reaching me. I listened intently as I heard a heart-felt message about the connections she had discovered between the two of us. She wanted to share with me her experiences with people I have loved but are no longer with me. Although I didn't realize it at the time, her words were heaven sent, and I was receiving an unexpected gift!

Tracey, whom I had never met, lived in the town where I had grown up and moved away from over fifty years ago. She had stumbled across my first book published a few years ago, *Lazarus Still Rises*, in a local store. I currently live in a state over five hundred miles away and had not ever been in the store where she found my book. Looking at the author's page, she discovered that I was the daughter of a local couple she had known many years ago. When a business card with my contact information tumbled out of the middle of the book, she was inspired to call me.

I could not wait to call her back. When we spoke, we agreed that her being able to contact me could only be orchestrated by the hand of God. Our Father really likes to thrill us by suddenly weaving invisible threads between us and total strangers!

Tracey told me she was the daughter of one of my high school classmates whom I had not seen since my graduation over fifty years ago. Her family lived near the small town where I grew up, and she had met my father who has now been gone for over thirty-five years. As a small child she accompanied her dad to visit his favorite high school teacher in his home.

My father taught Tracey's parents, who are now both deceased. Tracey recalled her mother saying many times, "I wish you could have had Mr. Spencer as a teacher. He made history come alive for his students!" I could appreciate that sentiment as Mr. Spencer's daughter and also as one who had been a student in his class. His love for teaching inspired me to also become a teacher. Tracy remembered seeing the marquee outside Van Buren High School after my father died. It said, "Thank you, Mr. Spencer." My father would have loved seeing that message, and Tracey seeing it and sharing that experience with me was an unexpected gift.

My "new" friend's conversation was filled with joy as she shared how much she loves the Lord and how He has blessed her life. Somehow, after finding my book and recognizing the memory stones we shared, she felt compelled to call me. After speaking with her I realized God was giving the two of us a special gift as he wove an invisible thread between us. He loves to bring believers who are total strangers together, so they can embrace each other in testimony. I really celebrate that when I experience it! God has some very unique ways of giving people, who have not previously met, memory stones to share. Sometimes, they just suddenly come without warning into our lives! That is one of His specialties.

Only a couple of weeks before my "new" friend called me, I had received in the mail a picture from one of my high school classmates. We had recently visited with each other at our high school reunion, and he mentioned he had a photograph I might like to see. When it arrived in the mail, I was stunned to see a picture of students from a one room elementary school taken over ninety years ago.

It was very common in those days for a small country school to have one teacher who taught all academic subjects for first through eighth grades. For the first time ever, I saw my father as a seven year old child, and the teacher standing with the class was his very own father. I had forgotten that my grandfather taught school for a few years. I remembered him as a hard-working farmer who used harnessed horses to plow the fields on his small farm, until his health failed him. Even though his being a teacher was a long-forgotten memory, I had never known he taught my father. God had coordinated the beautiful gifts of a conversation with a former classmate's daughter and a picture from long ago to enrich my soul! Thank you Father.

The Lord is extremely generous in the numerous ways He enriches believers' memories of loved ones who are no longer living. I once discovered a forgotten prayer book that had been given to me by a close friend, Betty, who had been gone for a few years. I found it the day after I came back from a three day spiritual retreat. I was experiencing a "mountain high," and then I found her book with a bookmark on the "Fourth Day".

The talk given on the last day of the retreat was centered on living out the rest of our lives with what we had experienced during that special time with the Lord. The title of the message was "The Fourth Day." Even though I had not seen Betty for many years, because she and her family had moved away a few years before she died, I could not escape recognizing the special timing of my rediscovering her book.

The Lord did that for me. He reconnected me with my

friend to remind me what I needed to do to continue living out my jubilation in being with Him. I remembered all the prayers Betty and I had shared together when we were young and our children, who are now in their forties, were very small. I could once again savor the time when we held hands and prayed aloud to our God whom we both loved. None of what was spoken and shared all those years ago had been lost. God was just refreshing all of that in my spirit!

Some of the spectacular memory stones God gives us come from unexpected encounters in nature. Recently, I shared with a friend about my sewing experiences from years ago. As we sat outside in her swing I told her how much I learned about perseverance from having to rip out misplaced seams and then redo them. I no more got the words out of my mouth, than she pointed to a spider above us which had just woven a beginning thread for its web, only to draw it back and start over! I absolutely love the way our Lord "talks" to us by giving us surprises to reveal to us that He is listening and watching us as we go about our daily lives. Only a Father who "spoils" His children would use a spider to give a visual demonstration of words His child has just spoken! Father, You are amazing!

One of my favorite unexpected encounters in nature came when my granddaughter Alyssa and I went to a nearby park to take the picture that appears on the cover of this book. Just before she stepped into the water to reach for one of the "memory stones", a butterfly greeted us and flew all around us. I had just finished my chapter on butterflies, and of course I had to take a picture of this friendly butterfly to include on the cover. Later, I realized the colors in the butterfly beautifully coordinated with the colors in Alyssa's top. Do you believe God does things like that! I know he did it just for us and now you can also enjoy our butterfly!

These unanticipated experiences are like "spiritual geysers" that just erupt so that we can have spectacular memory stones to cherish! He sends them to His children frequently in sudden, surprising ways like a geyser suddenly erupting to the delight of those who witness it.

Geysers are so fascinating, and we can even make some spiritual observations by studying them. History reveals that in 1870 the members of an expedition visited Yellowstone National Park in Wyoming. When they entered the Upper Geyser Basin, the first geyser they saw was one they named Old Faithful.

One of the explorers, Nathaniel P. Langford, shared his excitement about seeing something his group had never seen before! He shared how blessed they all were to come upon the geyser the very moment it was erupting. He described the thrill of seeing it erupt up close in the clear sunlight as an immense volume of clear, sparkling water projected one hundred and twenty-five feet into the air. Wow! God put on an unexpected show for them!

Today over one million eruptions have been recorded and the name, Old Faithful, is attributed to the fact that it is a highly predictable geothermal feature. It is not connected to any other thermal features of the Upper Geyser Basin. God just placed it there for people who can perceive His presence and be blessed by Him! God never changes. He is the same yesterday, today, and will be the same tomorrow. He is always faithful to us. Don't you just love it, that He gave us a memory stone like Old Faithful to remind us of that!

Upon further examining the history of the Old Faithful Geyser, I was surprised to discover this beautiful landmark was degraded for a period of time. In the early days of the park, it was often used as a laundry. Yes, I said laundry! Garments were placed in the crater so that when it erupted they were ejected, thoroughly washed.

Can you believe that is the value some placed on this awesome production by our God! The memory stone of seeing beautiful, rushing water over a hundred feet rise towards the sky and feeling the presence of God was forfeited for clean laundry!

It is just like mankind to take one of God's magnificent blessings and reduce its true value for a financial or current physical need. There is a lesson here to learn. Sometimes, we just don't see our God and therefore we miss savoring His awesomeness. We are just too distracted by things that are unimportant and temporary to see the eternal treasure in the unanticipated encounters He has sent.

I don't want to ever miss savoring God's awesomeness. Witnessing God provide unexpected encounters over the course of decades has caused a change in my personality - growing old does have some benefit! I used to be a shy withdrawn person in public places and now I have become an outgoing person who loves to talk to strangers. My joy from the Lord is overflowing, and His Spirit continually draws me to people I have never met before! I have been known to hug someone I just met in a department store after we spontaneously shared our love for the Lord. I never know when the Lord is going to do something new and exciting in the world around me. I just don't want to miss any of His surprises. I don't want to forfeit having amazing memory stones for the rest of my life, because I couldn't see God in action.

God does not fail to use every experience in our lives to weave together our tapestry of faith. Nothing is wasted by Him. Those daily events that bring sudden blessings from unexpected encounters are not just good luck. God has orchestrated them out of His loving generosity towards us. He keeps telling us to remember what He has done in our lives and share it with others. He wants us to notice them and not forget what He has done.

Our recalling of God's hand on our lives is where our true treasure lies on this side of eternity. Be prepared every day for the Holy Spirit to give you a sudden gift of joy! Remember to savor the days when His joy "sneaks up" on you, and then share it with others! These are not accidents. These are not coincidences. These are God's memory stones. Tell others what God did personally for you! Then they can also savor those memory stones with you!

Psalm 92:4,14

You thrill me, LORD with all you have done for me! I sing for joy because of what you have done.
Even in old age they will still produce fruit; they will remain vital and green.

Psalm 149:3

Praise his name with dancing, accompanied by tambourine and harp.

Zephaniah 3:17*

Yahweh your God is there with you, the warrior-Savior. He will rejoice over you with happy song. He will renew you by his love. He will dance with shouts of joy for you.

*New Jerusalem Bible

Chapter Nine

Memory Stones That Make Us Smile with Jesus

Our Lord really likes to give us memory stones to make us smile

Our Heavenly Father has a wonderful sense of humor and sometimes He likes to give us memory stones that not only make us smile but also make us laugh out loud. I really believe He laughs out loud with us in those moments. God is so exciting!

Almost fourteen years ago, my husband, who had sung in a trio on campus at Purdue University while he was a student there, began to sing again in public for the first time in forty years. He had stopped singing when he and his two friends graduated and went their separate ways. He didn't feel inspired to sing any more until he was baptized and joined our church at the age of sixty.

I like to say he was prayed into the church choir, because I absolutely believe a good friend who has been a member of the choir for many, many years did just that. Larry at first told

73

her "No" when she asked him to join, but he later changed his mind. I love it when the Holy Spirit leads us to change our minds, so we can receive the tremendous blessings God is waiting to give us!

When Larry first joined the choir, he said, "I'm struggling. My ability to sing is gone." However, the Lord was just giving him an opportunity to go it alone and see what it was like before He touched his voice in a miraculous way. After two years, Larry enthusiastically told me, "My voice is back. I can sing again!" Our grandchildren even observed that his singing was getting better and better. How's that for a critical, "impartial" evaluation that matters!

For the past several years Larry has presented music programs in our community using background tracks purchased online. He has performed at church programs, funerals, birthday parties, and wedding celebrations. He has even stood at grave sites and sung very moving Christian hymns a cappella. I've shed a few tears when I have seen Larry do all of this. I have seen the countenance of the Lord upon him during these times, and my gratitude for God doing this wells up in my spirit.

Larry loves country music and has just the right tone and range for this genre. His father was a big fan of this kind of music, so Larry grew up listening to many recordings of the old time country music stars. Larry also enjoys Hank Williams, Don Williams, Josh Turner, and Johnny Cash. He is such a big admirer of Johnny Cash's music that he has learned many of the songs he wrote. Frequently he introduces himself to his audience as "Johnny Crash." That always gets him a few smiles before he even begins to sing.

Larry once was asked to sing John Denver's song "Country Roads," at a very unusual occasion—the funeral of a good friend. Glenn loved that song and his wife Lois just knew it would bless her entire family if it was sung at his funeral. You should have seen all of us at this somber event in the sanctuary of our traditional church service singing so joyfully about "country roads that take us home." We knew Glenn had gone home to be with our Lord, and that he was now radiating in His presence. Knowing that, why not celebrate in the midst of our tears.

Larry was the perfect person to pull this off. I loved visualizing Jesus smiling as he stood next to Larry while he sang. Honestly, I can see our Lord singing with him. Our Lord certainly broke up a few funerals with unexpected joy when His feet walked this troubled earth. Remember the twelve year old daughter of Jairus who Jesus raised from the dead? *(Mark 5:37-41)* In Glenn's case we knew that he also had been touched by our Lord, and was alive and well with Him. We also know that someday we will be right there with Him. Knowledge of this gift of eternal life carries us in the midst of our sorrow to a wonderful place of hope and expectation for the future.

There is an interesting twist to Larry's story about artists he enjoys. If you had told me fifteen years ago that Larry would not only do solo performances in public, but would also imitate Elvis Presley, I would have felt very sorry for you and your current mental state. Now as I write these words "Elvis's white jacket" is hanging in the closet of my husband's study.

Larry has the perfect voice to sing many of Elvis's songs, and his heart was so much into this that he recently decided he needed the proper attire. Do you know how difficult it is these days to find a very inexpensive men's white formal jacket? Well, with my shopping genes at work, I rose to the occasion. Of course, the white jacket needed a few sequins and glitter added to transform it into something Elvis might have worn at one of his concerts. I just happen to love doing makeovers like that. However, I am still a little shocked that I was asked to do this by my retired veterinarian husband.

Larry added to this look by borrowing a piece of my favorite costume jewelry—a large gold chain necklace. I have worn this necklace for many occasions, but I never in my wildest dreams thought that I would someday be sharing it with Larry! He also purchased an Elvis wig and gold sunglasses. His singing is great, and when you see him in his full attire, you just have to have a good time watching him. You cannot believe how surprised his friends were the first time they saw him transform into "Elvis." I am sure our Lord laughs joyfully when He sees the result of His giving Larry his voice back after all these years.

This fun-soaked experience of Larry impersonating Elvis is a wonderful memory stone from God. Larry's face lights up when he sings the songs of Elvis, and when he sings the songs of many country artists. His face is especially radiant when he sings in the choir for the honor and glory of our God. All of these extraordinary moments came from our Lord. He foresaw how amazed people would be to see a retired veterinarian in his sixties suddenly begin an amateur singing career. He knew the great surprise people would have as they observed his voice continuing to improve instead of declining as he reached his seventies. Larry makes certain they know who is responsible. I think God just loves "showing off" like this. Isn't He amazing!

King David realized how awesome our living God is. He had the right idea about laughing, loving, singing and dancing with joy when he experienced His presence. Check out many of the Psalms David wrote. David composed at least half of the Psalms which were meant to be sung, not just read. Some Psalms speak about sorrow, fear, and the heaviness of life, but many reflect David's heart for God and the happiness he had in experiencing His character and His hand on his life.

David sometimes got so excited about God that he just had to dance. *2 Samuel 6:14* makes me smile every time I read it. *"And David danced before the LORD with all his might, wearing a priestly garment."* If David were alive today, I am sure he would have not had the slightest problem singing "Country Roads" in a church service to say good-bye to a friend. He might have even danced when he sung it. *Zephaniah 3:17* tells us that our

LORD even dances with us. David must have had company when he danced before the LORD, even if the people watching could not see it.

Don't squash your joy when it rises up in your spirit. Share it and become contagious. You have no idea who may be desperate to be "infected" that way. I have a wonderful friend who is in her eighties, and throughout their long marriage she and her husband have been avid dancers. Hazel and George honed their skills in the era of the fifties when young people knew how to do the jitterbug and other fun dances.

If you have watched the television show "Dancing with The Stars," you have seen several types of dances this wonderful couple has done. She and her husband frequently shared their joy of dancing with many people at church functions and other events. You just felt good inside when you watched them.

When Larry does some of his music programs, he asks people to get up and dance. Hazel and George have been at several of them, and they have made many people smile when they entered the dance floor. They contaminated everyone watching with their infectious joy!

George and Hazel may have slowed down slightly in the last couple of years, but they are both still just as young at heart and joyful as ever. Hazel stood next to my table recently at a church dinner and said, "Let's dance!" I am the most uncoordinated person you would ever want to meet, but I briefly followed her command. Believe me, if she asked you to do the same, you would want to dance. I tell her every time I see her, "Don't stop dancing! Remember *Zephaniah 3:17!*"

The Lord has released something in Larry, George, and Hazel's spirits. He has set them free from inhibitions that would otherwise prevent them from using their gifts and keep them from experiencing His joy. His Hand is upon them in a way that gives others memory stones of pleasure for their lives.

I am very entertained by the reality shows where some amateur singers stand before a national audience for the first time to demonstrate their talent. Until their audition, many of these people had never sung before a large audience. When they reveal their beautiful voices and the audience cheers, they respond by crying. I cry with these contestants, because it is so moving to see them realize their God-given gifts. It just seems to be so freeing to them. I experience that same emotion when I watch Larry sing and Hazel and George dance. I shed tears of joy!

Everyone has "music" inside of them that has been placed there by the living God. The music may result in their singing or dancing, or something else, but it is there waiting to be expressed. Release it, and you will make someone else's heart "sing!" You definitely have something special in you that the Lord is waiting for you to recognize and share.

God can use you to make memory stones that feed the souls of others. Don't be afraid. Don't hesitate. Share yourself and Jesus will stand beside you smiling. Maybe, He will even be dancing beside you. Who would want to miss that!

"Elvis" crooning to beloved senior citizens.

"Elvis's" jacket

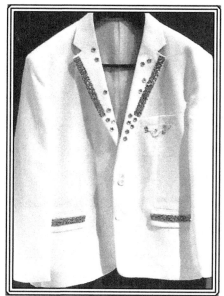

George and Hazel Sniff

What are your gifts?

† Are you a writer? Don't say no too quickly. Do you write emails, texts, or comments on face book? If you do, you are a writer. Write to someone today who needs to be uplifted. Consider writing your thoughts in a journal and see where the Lord takes you. Use your words today to bless someone.

† Do you frequently make people laugh because you have said something humorous? Share your humor wherever you can. Not every person has to enjoy your humor. You have no idea what laughter does to soothe the pain of a hurting heart. People need this kind of sunshine in their lives. You may be the person today that brings it to them.

† Are you a good listener? There are so many lonely people in this world who need someone who has a good listening ear and cares about them. Ask people you meet about their lives. Let them share some of themselves with you. Be Jesus to them today. He is the best listener there ever was.

† Do you like to read? Do you frequently tell others about a good book you recently read? Some of my favorite books came to me, because someone took time to tell me about them. Of course, the best book in the entire universe is God's Word. Read it every day and you will have something spectacular to share with others.

† Do you like to cook? Have you shared something you have prepared with someone who may be under the weather in body or spirit? Numerous people today rarely enjoy home cooked meals. If you have this talent, you will be appreciated whenever you share it with others. Jesus fed others and you can also.

† Are you comfortable praying aloud? Have you asked someone lately if you could pray with them? Most people whom you ask are extremely grateful. It is not so much your words but your heart for Jesus that will soothe the ache they have inside of them. Jesus is listening for your words and rejoices when He hears them.

All of what I have mentioned here are just some of the "music" that the Lord has given to His children. He wants you to share "your song" with others. The wonderful thing about you doing this, it releases your spirit to feel the pleasure of the Lord upon you. Nothing in the world feels better!

Jacie Snipes, my granddaughter, drew this picture of Laughing Jesus.

Song of Solomon 2:11-12*

Behold, the winter is past; the rain is over and gone. The flowers appear on the earth, the time of singing has come, and the voice of the turtledove is heard in our land.

Isaiah 61:11**

For as the earth bursts with spring wildflowers, and as a garden cascades with blossoms, so the Master, GOD, brings righteousness into full bloom and puts praise on display before the nations.

**The Message

Revelation 4:3*

And he who sat there had the appearance of jasper and carnelian, and around the throne was a rainbow that had the appearance of an emerald.

*English Standard Version

Chapter Ten

Memory Stones from Flowers

God used iris flowers as a memory stone of hope for our family

My mother absolutely loved roses and tried for many years to plant rose bushes. Her older sister Frances had a "green thumb" and had them flourishing all over her yard. She would give advice to Mother about growing them, and Mother would try unsuccessfully to replicate her success. We would enjoy a few roses for a couple of years, but then they died off. I think they just needed more attention than Mother had time to provide.

Frances had graduated from college with a degree in science, but had decided against a career to be a stay at home mom. Even with seven children, she found time in the spring and summer to attend to her flourishing gardens of flowers and vegetables. Mother, who was a full time registered nurse with three children, simply wasn't inclined to spend much of her free time gardening. She did however enjoy other outdoor

85

activities.

Mother's moments outside happened mainly on her days off when she hung laundry on a clothes line and then retrieved it later. I still remember the fragrant smell of sun-dried sheets. There were moments of celebration on laundry day when our beds were freshly made. I saw that joy in Mother in the midst of her toil.

Many summers my father planted a garden, and Mother prepared sumptuous meals from what was harvested. She also loved to go into the woods and hunt for edible mushrooms. When she was successful, she was as excited as if she had found a pot of gold! Those mushrooms made some of the most delicious meals I ever had!

Still, God made sure that Mother had her flowers in the midst of all her other efforts for her family. Purple Iris flowers grew faithfully outside her kitchen window every year. These flowers flourished no matter what the conditions seemed to be. They just didn't require the tender loving care that her roses seemed to need. The Iris plant bloomed every spring and unfurled its stunning flowers. It seemed to say, "Here we are! Enjoy!"

All the inhabitants of God's creation have been blessed with an encouraging message of hope from His flowers. There are stories about many different kinds of flowers, and the Iris has its own intriguing story. In Greek, the name "Iris" translates as "rainbow," which is one iris definition. Many people assume that "rainbow" refers to the many colors this flower comes in, but the root of the meaning traces to Greek mythology, where a Greek goddess named Iris delivered messages for the gods from the underworld. She would travel along rainbows as she moved between heaven and earth.

As intriguing as this story is in Greek Mythology, the Book of Revelation in chapter four gives a more thrilling one about messages being sent from heaven to earth. In this Scripture John describes the rainbow which encircles God's throne and the messenger is God Himself. God not only employs rainbows to give us messages of hope, but He also uses living things throughout creation to speak to us. I really enjoy the idea that somehow God planted the Iris plant in our family's front yard to remind us of His continuing presence no matter what sadness came to our family.

Actually, I think God put the Iris plant in our yard to especially comfort my mother. Her heart was crushed as she watched my brother, who had been bedridden for three years, die at the age of nine of an undiagnosed illness. Seeing the flowers blooming every spring was a special message of hope for our family. I have not been blessed to have them in any of the places I have lived for the past fifty years, but I have not forgotten seeing them all the years I was growing up. God spoke to me through those flowers.

I love it that God has spoken to many others through Irises. Another story behind the Iris flower is the one of the Fleur-de-Lis. Throughout the middle ages, this symbol was seen by some as an Iris, and it came to symbolize Christianity. In 496 A.D. a Christian queen named Clotilde, who was credited with spreading Christianity to the western world, may have started the tradition of using the symbol on flags and banners. Castles throughout the French and English countryside soon followed in representing the Trinity. Reading about this historical footnote makes me appreciate even more seeing this flower take up residence outside our home when I was growing up.

The appreciation of this flower remains prevalent all over the world. Today, gardeners find the iris flowers to be very attractive, and they multiply quickly, enhancing every garden. Christianity parallels this for the world. Wherever Christians reside, they bless the people around them. For many gardeners the fleur-de-lis/Iris is seen as a symbol of friendship—perhaps it symbolizes friendship with God for those who see Him in their gardens.

This plant is also an enduring perennial, and God knew we

needed this symbol of His enduring love. Perhaps, that helps to explain why people are so drawn to it. The Iris is a subject of poetry, paintings, and countless garden photographs. The Victorian era language of flowers said it represented faith, hope, courage, wisdom and admiration. The sword-like leaves were said to mimic the sorrows that pierced Mary's heart as she watched her son Jesus suffer and die. Whatever the symbolism represented by these flowers, they were meant to bless our family. They did. Thank you, Father.

Mother moved away from her Iris flowers when she and Dad sold their home many years ago. Then the year after my Dad died, she left everything she had ever known in her home state of Indiana to be close to my family here in Georgia. Several years ago, the home where I grew up was torn down. It was thirty to forty years old when my parents purchased it, and was always needing some repair work and remodeling. I am guessing the last owners felt it was more efficient to tear it down and start over. It was difficult to know how many families had lived in our home prior to us. How many years did they enjoy the Iris flowers? The faithful Iris plant disappeared when the house was destroyed. It had done its job. It was sent by the Lord to encourage a family and be a memory stone of hope. The flowers are gone, but the message they brought is not. It remains forever with me.

A few years ago, I found a ceramic pitcher and bowl in a thrift store. What drew me to stand and gaze at this decorative set were the Iris flowers painted boldly on the pitcher. I brought it home, and placed it in my dining room as a reminder of the Iris memory stone my heavenly Father had given our family. Later, I gave the set to a friend after her husband died. I told her my family story about the Iris plant and the story of hope it brought. I also told her I was passing it on to her as a message of hope and encouragement. At first she said she could not accept this gift, because it was so special to me. I told her, "You must, because the gift of hope is one that grows and blesses you, only if you pass it on."

Many years ago, a lovely lady at our church named Iris knew about the message of hope that could only come from the Lord. She lived it all of her over seventy years, and left a treasure of testimony for her family. She also left her Bible with all kinds of personal notes in the margins about her walk with the Lord. At her funeral, family members read some of her favorite Scripture and the comments she had written. She knew how to pass on the "Iris message of hope."

I am trying to pass this message on to my family. For some time I have had another Iris memory stone in my dining room. It is a large framed print of Iris flowers. When I first saw it in a store many years ago, I felt nostalgia sweep over me. I felt like I was back in the yard of the home where I grew up. I purchased the print and placed it in my dining room. Recently, I placed a white wicker storage chest containing toys for my grandchildren under it. They see the promise of the Iris every time they get a toy.

This message of promise became complete when I recently had my mother's portrait painted by a local artist. She used the photograph of Mother's ninetieth birthday, which reminded me of the joy my family felt when we celebrated it five years before her death. Mother told me that day, "I feel like a queen!" I hung my beautiful Mother's picture in the dining room. Now she and her flowers of encouragement have been united.

God is leaving us memory stones of hope and encouragement every day. He knows when we ache, when we grieve, when we despair. He seeks to hold us in His arms. Look around you at the beauty He has put in your path. He puts it there just for you! Celebrate it and share this with others. Don't let them miss the spectacular moments and memory stones that the living God gives you! Celebrate His Holy Name! Praise Him!

Poem by **Iris Spruill***

I see a thousand miracles,
With each new holy dawn.
A swiftly fading memory
Of yesterdays now gone.

I shall not dwell upon the past,
I must be moving on.
I feel God's love enfolding me;
I feel it make me strong.

I feel it lifting up my soul
Above the doubt and wrong.
And I obey Him as I run
To sing the world His song.

*This poem was shared at Iris's funeral.

Fleur-De-Lis

Iris, a hardy plant with beautiful colored flowers,
And so easy to grow!
Just like God is so easy to know!

Iris, a Greek word for rainbow;
Bearer of blossoms with hues of yellow, white, violet, and
blue,
Showing God's promise that He is here for you!

Iris leaves last throughout the seasons
And you can count on the flowers to return in summer's sun,
When winter is done!

The blossom of the iris is a three part flower,
Just like God is three in one: Father, Holy Spirt,
And, Jesus Christ His only Son.

Iris do not require constant care,
Only soil, sun, rain and air,
And for your delight they will be there!

Just like God wants you to have joy, day and night!
So trust and do not fear,
Iris will every year appear,
Just like God, year after year, holds you near!

Loretta Vickers*
July 2017

*Loretta Vickers is also the artist who drew the Iris illustration for this chapter. She is a long time educator, artist, poet, and my friend of almost forty years. I am so blessed by her!

Matthew 16:24-25*

Then Jesus told his disciples, "If anyone would come after me, let him deny himself and take up his cross and follow me. For whoever would save his life will lose it, but whoever loses his life for my sake will find it."

*English Standard Version

Chapter Eleven

Memory Stones of Crosses

The world needs God's memory stones of crosses

As the mourners made their way to the family cemetery to lay to rest this wonderful husband, father, and grandfather, they were greeted by three white, connected crosses in the sky. Then as they were all getting out of their cars to gather around the grave, they looked up in the sky again and saw they had been greeted by a huge white cross! Just to make sure the mourners recognized the source of these memory stones, the Holy Spirit showed up as a soft gentle breeze to touch the faces of those grieving.

The day after the funeral and burial, Lamar's beloved wife opened her front door and there to greet her in the morning sky was another huge cross. Our amazing God was showing off!

Lamar loved making wooden crosses and gave them away by the hundreds because his generous spirit was overflowing with love for his Lord! Now the Lord was returning the favor and letting the crosses appear in the heavenly sky as a gift from a beloved man to his grieving wife, family, and friends.

Accompanying these visual gifts of splendor were the gifts of peace and overflowing love in his wife's heart. She had been at his side constantly to care for him and love him through his suffering and tremendous pain during the thirty-five years of their marriage. In the last months of his life, she sent daily emails to their hundreds of friends asking for prayer and giving testimony about the continuous answers to those prayers that swept through their home from the hand of the living God.

Joy that can only come from the Lord permeated their home as they strived to live fully each day. Physical, emotional, and spiritual pain can draw us so deeply inward that our focus is entirely on ourselves. Not so for Lamar and Lynn. During their years together they frequently took food to others who were in need and offered themselves in whatever ways were needed. They loved people, and they loved the Lord!

They both had been gifted with musical talent from the hand of God. Lamar played several instruments and even played drums in a band from the age of fourteen to the age of forty. Being extremely creative, Lamar, after leaving the band, transformed one of his drums into a light fixture. (Are you smiling about that? I am!)

Lynn, being gifted with a beautiful, powerful voice, sings out in full spirit for the Lord. She just lights up with joy when she sings to Him! God placed His music inside both of them, and it spilled out as they shared it with the world. People just feel good to be around those who are like them.

In the last few weeks of Lamar's life, he insisted that Lynn follow through with her commitment to be the spiritual director of a four day women's Christian retreat. He even went into a hospice facility during this time, so the two of them could partner with Christ to lead others to Him. They lived the message of the cross and their testimony gave many, many people memory stones of hope.

Almost six years ago prior to his death, Lamar made his

first cross as an afterthought from leftover wood he had used to build a cedar swing for Lynn. Lamar could always see the beauty in items that others would throw away. Isn't that just like our Lord, who chose not to throw us away, to give this gift of perception to one of His children!

When others admired Lynn's cross, Lamar felt the need to begin making more of them and giving them away. He made these beautiful hand held crosses from dogwood, oak, and maple. No one could pay him for what the Lord had laid on his heart to do. He was giving Jesus away with each cross. He did not keep track of where his crosses went- their destination was being tracked by the living God. The Lord knew where the receptive hearts were and placed the crosses in the hands of these believers.

Using trees from their two hundred acres of land, Lamar built a huge cross standing twenty feet tall and placed it near their cabin. They called this vacation cabin their "Po House." Then some distance away he built another large cross that was over twelve feet tall. He put this one on a hill and turned the area into a place of worship for the family. Many Easter Sunrise services took place there.

The land where these two crosses stand has been anointed not only by the prayers of Lamar and his family, but also by the generations before them. Lamar and Lynn's children are the sixth generation to own this land. These six generations are not the first families to inhabit this property. The hundreds of arrowheads that have been found on this site give a window back in time to hundreds of years ago when Indian tribes settled there.

Only our living God knows how many people through the ages have worshiped Him on the sacred ground where Lamar's crosses now rest. When I visited this site with Lynn, I picked up one of the stones at the foot of his cross on the hill. This memory stone rests on the Bible along with the cross that you see on every Scripture page of this book.

The cross lying on the Bible in the Scripture pages was made by my brother-in-law, John, who lives a few hundred miles from us in a small town in Indiana. He is married to my husband Larry's sister, Lana. John also, like Lamar, makes crosses so he can give Jesus away to others. He has made thousands of them, and like Lamar he will not allow anyone to pay him. His and Lamar's stories are similar in that when people first see these crosses which fit in the palm of the hand, they yearn to have one for themselves. They are drawn to Jesus when they see a cross, and somehow holding one in their hands is like holding Jesus Himself.

John has been making his crosses for over twenty years and people call him the "Cross Man." John remembers reading a book many years ago about the symbolism of the cross and the words remained with him: "The cross is a visible symbol of the invisible power of Christ." We are eternally thankful that our Lord went to the cross to redeem us, and provide for us to be with Him when our earthly time is completed. When we hold a cross in our hands, we remember the power of our Lord which the world cannot grasp.

Thousands of stories about the crosses made by John and Lamar have been written in God's kingdom records. Perhaps, Lamar is having a conversation with our Lord about them right now. John knows only a few of the stories, but those are enough for him to feel compelled to keep giving Jesus away.

Our Lord let John, with his obedient heart, be encouraged by seeing some of the good that was done by his giving away the crosses. One day when John was in a waiting room of a hospital, he saw a lady he had never met stand up as her name was called. She opened her hand and revealed what she had been holding. It was one of John's crosses made from red oak. It was unique in several ways, and he recognized it. John says he knows "his crosses!" Jesus smiled on him that day to give him confirmation He was pleased with him. It was as if he said, "See how you are blessing so many people who you have never met." Don't you just love it when Jesus does that for us! He loves us so very much, and He just wants to "spoil" us from time to time!

John also remembers recognizing another one of his crosses. On that occasion he was at a friend's funeral, and he saw that the cross he had made for his friend was resting against the open lid of his coffin. When his friend had lain dying from an advanced stage of cancer, there was only one thing he wanted- his cross. The family knew he would want it to be present in the funeral home as they all said goodbye. They said, "He's crossing Jordan with his cross." I am sure that made our Lord smile when he heard those words. How many people saw the cross on the casket and felt a stirring in their hearts? I am sure there were several, for that is how the Holy Spirit works among us.

John's own mother, who loved the Lord with her whole heart, held one of his crosses in her hands as her body lay in her casket. Even as her spirit had gone home to be with the Lord, she was still giving testimony on this side of eternity. The message given by the memory stone crosses is so profound that no one can ignore seeing it. They can ignore believing it and accepting it, but they cannot ignore its presence in the world.

John and Lamar are joined by another "Cross Man," John Packwood, a photographer and filmmaker. He is a member of the Tuckston United Methodist Church, and it is in this sanctuary that he received a special message from the Lord. He noticed the large golden cross suspended from a wooden rafter of the sanctuary frequently created unusual shadows. These shadows changed shape as different lights were directed onto them from various angles.

One Sunday John saw something remarkable. The shadow created that day looked like arms drooping downward. John believed this shadow was a reflection of the sorrow over the crucifixion of Jesus. He realized he was seeing something the

Holy Spirit was directing, and he took a photograph of this stunning sight so he could share it with others.

John also received an unspoken message for which he absolutely takes no credit. He says the words are totally different from how he usually expresses his thoughts, and he knows they were given to him from the Holy Spirit. Did the writers of the books of the Bible feel the same as they recorded the Word of God? Have you ever expressed thoughts so profound and different from what you normally share that you feel God Himself has touched your spirit? These are very thrilling experiences to joyously savor.

This is John's message about the cross with the drooping arms: "The Cross of Salvation stands firm with the glow of hope for Christians. But, always in the background is the shadow with its arms weighed down in sorrow. We must never forget the pain and suffering of the cross of crucifixion from which the joy of salvation rises." Both the framed photograph of the cross John saw that day, and the plaque bearing the inspired words given to him by the Holy Spirit hang in the narthex of the church. Every time someone walks by and sees these gifts from the Holy Spirit, John is also giving Jesus away through the memory stone of the cross.

Three men who love Jesus have given Him away with memory stones of His cross. None of these men would allow anyone to pay them for what Jesus freely gave to the world. Won't you join them and give Jesus away? Give Him to someone in your family who hasn't yet found Him, to a friend who needs to experience the victory of Jesus in his life, or to a complete stranger whom the Lord sends to you!

The crosses you give away can be built of materials other than wood. They can be built in your hearts and spirits and delivered by the words given to you by the Holy Spirit. Take up your cross and follow Jesus with joy. Share Him with the generosity of your words, deeds, and prayers. Be a "cross man or cross woman" for Christ! Love Him all the way into eternity!

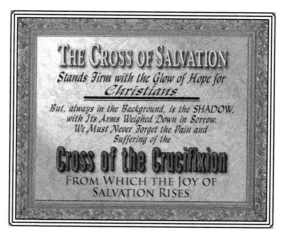

Caption: These Gifts from the Holy Spirit hang in the foyer
of Tuckston United Methodist Church.

Thank you, John Packwood.

102

Lamar gave away hundreds of
these small crosses.

Lamar Coffeen's cross on a hill—an anointed place of worship.

103

Psalm 56:8

You keep track of all my sorrows. You have collected all my tears in your bottle. You have recorded each one in your book.

Psalm 100:4*

Enter his gates with thanksgiving, and his courts with Praise! Give thanks to him; bless his name!

* English Standard Version

Chapter Twelve

My Writing Table is a Memory Stone

The Lord can make a memory stone out of anything we touch

I love to imagine the things Jesus made with His carpentry skills. Did he build furniture for His Mother Mary? Did He make her a table at which His family sat and enjoyed meals together before He began His ministry? What happened to all the things he touched and created with His hands? Did He sing and pray over all He built? Wouldn't you have loved sitting in a wood chair He had made and that had been anointed by His Spirit? I can't even imagine having something in my hands He had touched.

There is something spiritual about holding an item once owned by a loved one who is now gone. I have my mother's case for her glasses which her hands held every day for over thirty years. She carefully placed her glasses in this dark brown case every night and retrieved them the first thing every morning. This storage box for her glasses made several trips to the hospital and was always near her bedside.

How can something so common be something so magnificent to me? Her hands having touched her glasses case hundreds of times made it priceless to me. Sometimes I just rub my hands over it and tell her I love her and miss her. When she was living, I didn't realize the simple things she owned would be my treasure when she was gone. I didn't know they would become memory stones from her.

Yes, I am extremely sentimental. I believe our Lord is sentimental too. Scripture says our God keeps our tears in bottles. Can you believe He cares that much about us! What touches our spirit touches His! A grieving friend recently said she hopes He doesn't run out of bottles for our tears. Me too!

A couple of years ago I decided to get rid of my large bulky desk which had always become uncomfortable when I used my computer for long periods of time. It looked pretty in the store when I bought it, but it was never meant to be used for hours and hours of productive computer time. I would have paid the people who came to take it off my hands just for getting it out of my study, but fortunately they were happy to get it free.

I searched the local furniture stores for desks that would be large enough to accommodate my computer, reference materials, and all the other things I seem to need when I am writing. I was definitely avoiding pretty over practical. Mother would have been so proud of me! Even though she is not physically here, her past words of advice are definitely still "raising" me at my tender age. (Some of us just take longer to mature!)

I knew I would be writing *God's Memory Stones* at this new desk, and so I asked the Lord to go shopping with me. I wished I had done more of that in the past. I would have more of Him in my house, instead of so much "stuff." (Every time I take another load to a thrift store, my husband says, "Another teaspoon out of the ocean!") However, nothing I found seemed to be the right desk for me to use for this special time with my Lord.

Finally, I found a delightful store which housed home décor and lovely furniture that had been refurbished or personally built by the owner's husband. I was intrigued with the name "Brand New Thing/ Paint with Class," and I just knew it was going to be a blessed experience shopping there. As soon as I walked into the store, I felt the presence of the Lord. He was all over the place! Merchandise was carefully placed throughout the store, and mingled in with so many beautiful things was written Scripture. I saw a piece of framed blackboard with the words, "Enter His Gates with Thanksgiving and His courts with praise." I felt that I had just entered into a place that the Lord had touched with His own hands. (That wonderful framed Scripture from the store is now in my prayer room!)

I looked around carefully and was drawn to a pine farm table with beautiful oak legs which had been painted in a light grey. A glaze had been added to make it look like a very old piece. I really enjoy furniture that has the character of age. I also appreciate talented people who can take pieces that are new and transform them in a way that gives them the appearance of something from another era. Then too, I don't mind adding to the character of a piece of furniture by letting it experience the natural wear and tear of being in my home. (After all, I have eight grandchildren to help with this!)

I discovered that the owner's name is Martha, and since that was my Mother's name, I was delighted to talk to someone with the same name. You don't meet many women with that name today! I was also pleased to discover that the owner's husband had made this table. It was one of the first ones of this design that he had done. I realized that moving the lower center board, which connected the two sides, back enough to give me ample leg room would convert this farm table into a desk. I was drawn to it for reasons I could not explain, and I couldn't wait to have it delivered to my freshly painted study.

After I purchased this desk, I asked Martha about the experience her husband had in making it. Sometimes the Holy Spirit makes us curious enough to ask questions that lead us into discovering something special about what we are experiencing.

How many times have you been with complete strangers and just opened your mouth to ask them questions, and they reveal the most interesting details that totally enrich your conversation with them? You learn something new and unusual, because you are focused in an outward direction!

I discovered that Martha and her husband had prayed repeatedly over my new desk as it was being made. They "baked" prayers into the place where my hands and computer would rest. She also told me that as her husband was building it, he frequently stopped to ask the Lord to help him figure out how to do the next step. I am doing this also as I search for the message of hope the Lord wants me to share with you. The Lord guided the hands of this carpenter who knew Him intimately. Hearing of how my new desk was built confirmed for me that I was meant to use it for writing this book. My mother's hands touching her glasses case made it special to me, and the Lord's "touching" my writing desk made it anointed for me. I delight in the Lord making those connections for me!

Later, I learned that though the store's original name was "Paint with Class," they decided that "Brand New Thing" was the name they were transitioning to. This new name came from Scripture they had written on a huge blackboard in the center room of the store. It was: *Isaiah 43:18-20 "See I am about to do a brand new thing. I have already begun! I will make a pathway through the wilderness for my people to come home. I will create rivers for them in the desert…So that my chosen people can be refreshed."* I loved the gift of a new desk being bathed in the promise of Scripture, and especially one that gave the hope of God doing a brand new thing in my life.

In all the hours that I sat at my desk on my computer, I came to the realization that the Lord had touched something besides my new desk. He had given me the presence of mind to realize something significant about where I sat. My desk faces a wall that is shared by my prayer room. On the other side of this wall is my Great Aunt Nora's writing table. Just as she sat at her desk and wrote words of inspiration to others, I am following her on the other side of the time continuum, and I am seeking to do the same.

Perhaps, my desk will someday reside in the home of a family member and be a memory stone just as Great Aunt Nora's desk is for me. Wherever it resides, may it be used it in some way that blesses others. The path for this piece of family history is totally in the hands of our Lord.

I pray that every generation of my family will share themselves and their words with others in a way that will glorify the Lord. May He touch everything in their lives which matters for His kingdom, and may they live victoriously all of their days. The hands of The Carpenter will lead them.

Wherever you go, whatever you purchase, or whom-
ever you meet, ask the Lord to go before you and touch
all of those places, situations, and people. If you do that,
your hands will touch where He has been! Be sure and
share these encounters with your family and friends, so
they will be encouraged to find these same paths with
our Lord. Give Him the honor and glory! He is so AWE-
SOME!

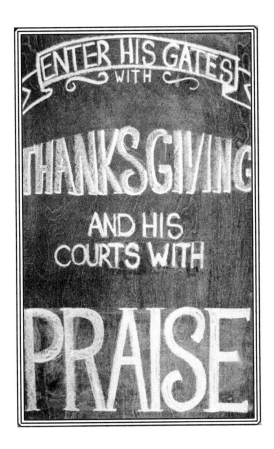

Isn't this what we all want to do?
Seeing you do this can be a memory stone for those you love!

Isaiah 60:13

The glory of Lebanon will be yours, the forests of cypress, fir, and pine to beautify my sanctuary. My temple will be glorious!

Chapter Thirteen

A Memory Stone Made for God's Glory

God's craftsman created a podium to honor a life and to give God the glory

God saw it long before it came into existence. When I go to church and enter the room, there it is to greet me. It is a beautiful, hand built, cherry wood podium with words burned into the front which dedicate it to the memory of my Mother. She sat in this room for over thirty years as a member of a Sunday school class, and for several years now, I have also been there as a member of another class. I am there without her, but I am never without the memory of her. This piece of furniture is a wonderful memory stone for me to cherish.

Love for the Lord and blessed hands built this podium. This is the place where our teachers rest their notes and Bibles when they stand behind the podium and share their inspiration for that Sunday's lesson. I have had the privilege of being there myself, and I feel God's presence every time.

This podium is just one of many pieces of furniture that have been built for our church by a recently retired professor, Gene Pesti, who just happens to love woodworking, and singing every week in our church choir. His grandfather, who was born in 1890 and died the year before Gene was born, was a cabinet maker from Hungary. He came to the United States when he was a young man. He opened a cabinet shop in Cleveland, Ohio and enjoyed his craft for many years. Gene fell in love with woodworking when he took an industrial arts class in junior high school. Gene's love for working with wood has continued throughout his entire life. His grandfather would have been so proud to see Gene's treasuring the legacy of woodworking.

The gorgeous cherry wood for the podium was donated by another generous man who also sings in our choir. Ray Lewis had been given the wood by family members who own a saw mill. He had been storing it in a shed, and he just knew that his professor friend would have a wonderful use for it. I am sure God directed this very kind man's heart in making the decision to give away wood that would become something so beautiful.

Gene felt a calling to make something pleasing to the Lord from what he was given. I believe even before the wood was cut, it had been anointed by the Lord. He knew it was to be used in His house for His honor and glory. Gene has built several pieces for worship at our church. He has made large crosses, a pulpit, portable altar rails with kneeling benches, and other beautiful pieces. He has used cedar, pine, and cherry wood to make all of these things. He has made them all out of his love for doing things with his hands in a way that blesses the worship of others. His heart for worship is not only revealed in his singing, but in the gifts his hands bring forth.

Gene's first step in making something out of wood is visualizing what the piece will look like. Once he can see it, he draws his own plan and cuts the wood pieces. He then fits the pieces together like a puzzle to see what adjustments are needed. He sometimes needs to learn a new skill to complete a project he has not done before. He finds that when this happens, it makes the whole experience more interesting and creative. God just loves to take us down a new path, and Gene enjoys this so much!

When I talk with Gene about the spiritual journey he travels as he prepares wood for the dedicated use of worship in God's house, I wonder, "Was the journey similar for other craftsmen of sacred objects of worship through the ages? What about those who prepared King Solomon's temple? What did they think about the enormity of their assignment?" This temple was built 480 years after the Israelites left Egypt. For all this time they did not have a permanent place to worship God. God's temple was to be built only in His timing, by whom He chose, and only by His direction.

Those who were experts in woodworking were very important to the work of building the temple. Gold, as well as wood, was used in very prominent ways. We read in *1 Kings Chapter 5* about the contribution of King Hiram of Tyre. He had always been a loyal friend of King Solomon's father, King David, and so King Solomon asked him to provide cedar from Lebanon. King Hiram told him that not only would he provide him with cedar, he would also give him cypress wood.

Cypress and cedar wood were used throughout the temple. This included two cypress folding doors at the entrance and the inner courtyard which had cedar beams after every three layers of hewn stone. Olive wood was also used to make two cherubim, the doors to the entrance to the inner sanctuary, and the doorposts for the entrance to the Temple. King Solomon enlisted 30,000 laborers from Israel to get the timber. He also used 70,000 common laborers, 80,000 stonecutters, and 3,600 others to supervise the work of building the temple. Every one of these thousands of people worked with materials that were touched by the Spirit of the living God.

King Solomon asked for a man named Huram to come

from Tyre to build the furnishings and utensils for the Temple. *Chapter 7 of 1 Kings* tells us about the extensive, elaborate work of this man. He was an expert craftsman and only someone anointed by the Lord could have possibly been entrusted for this work.

In *Chapter 8 of 1 Kings* we see that after all the work was completed, the temple and everything in it was dedicated. I cannot even imagine how thrilled the Israelites must have been, when after seven years of labor, they saw that the temple was finally completed! After The Ark of the LORD's covenant was put into the inner sanctuary of the Temple, they saw the pleasure of the living God when His glorious presence came as a cloud and filled the Temple!

Sadly, King Solomon's temple was destroyed almost four hundred years after it was built. Seventy years later a smaller temple was built to replace it, and this temple was standing when Jesus walked the earth. The first one was filled with the glory of the Lord, and this second temple was the one that was blessed by His physical presence! When this second temple was built a few hundred years before Christ, those who remembered the original temple actually wept. They saw it was not nearly as grand as the original. They had no idea that the God of our universe would actually walk in this temple as the Lord Jesus Christ!

It is the presence of God in our houses of worship that makes them so spectacular. He can anoint craftsmen today to do the same work that the craftsmen did for King Solomon's temple. All of the furnishings made today can also be touched by His Spirit and be made sacred. When we dedicate our worship in our churches to Him, His glory can again fill our sanctuaries.

I love it that people like Gene, who made so many wonderful pieces for our church, including a podium in memory of someone who also loved the Lord, are used by our God. Gene's use of old world cedar for the baptismal fount for our church, his use of other kinds of wood, and his attention to detail make me believe he has a connection with craftsmen throughout the ages. He and all of those who have used their hands in this way have surely felt the pleasure of the Lord upon them. It is obvious that there is a special joy for them when they use their very own hands to build those things that are used for worship of our living God.

Gene speaks about his experiences of visiting churches in Europe that are hundreds of years old. He always says a prayer for the wooden structures, candle stands, pulpits and other pieces that are in place. His fervent desire is that people be blessed in their journey of faith by what they see when they worship in the midst of the blessed things of Christ. Perhaps, Gene's prayer is the same as the one that has been offered by all of God's craftsmen throughout the ages.

I love reading about the building of King Solomon's temple, and all the beautiful, consecrated objects that were built by craftsmen to be used in worship in the very place where the living God presided. God touches and anoints everything that has been built and put in place by human hands for His glory. God Himself must have seen all the materials and people who touched them thousands of years before they came into place to prepare His temple. I also believe that everything built today and put into place for worship was seen by Him thousands of years before those now living came into this world.

The podium Gene built came to be because our friend Ray donated the wood. It was dedicated and prayed over the day it came to rest in a Sunday school classroom. What will its journey be through the years? The cherry wood darkens in a stunning way as it ages, becoming more attractive in a deeper, richer way. That is a wonderful analogy to what happens to us as we worship our God. Our spirits become deeper and richer in a way that pleases Him. Perhaps we even become memory stones for our God and that makes Him smile.

Thank you Gene Pesti for Mother's podium.

Luke 22:17-20

Then he took a cup of wine and gave thanks to God for it. Then he said, "Take this and share it among yourselves. For I will not drink wine again until the kingdom of God has come." He took some bread and gave thanks to God for it. Then he broke it in pieces and gave it to the disciples, saying, "This is my body, which is given for you. Do this to remember me. After supper he took another cup of wine and said, "This cup is the new covenant between God and his people—an agreement confirmed with my blood, which is poured out as a sacrifice for you."

Revelation 22:1-3

Then the angel showed me a river with the water of life, clear as crystal, flowing from the throne of God and of the Lamb. It flowed down the center of the main street. On each side of the river grew a tree of life, bearing twelve crops of fruit, with a fresh crop each month. The leaves were used for medicine to heal the nations. No longer will there be a curse upon anything, for the throne of God and of the Lamb will be there, and his servants will worship him.

Chapter Fourteen

Memory Stones Borne by Christmas Trees

Our decorated Christmas trees can tell the story of Jesus

As I knelt at the altar on this communion Sunday in February, I thought about Jesus and His beloved disciples having the Last Supper together only hours before He was crucified. He fervently wanted them to experience this time of fellowship in a way that would enable them to understand and remember what was about to happen. He was soon to give the gift of Himself in exchange for their eternal lives and for the eternal lives of all who would accept Him. Now, I was replicating this same experience with Jesus. In my moments at the altar with Him, a special memory stone awaited me.

As I prepared to take the offering of bread and grape juice to remind me of my Lord's sacrifice, I spotted a small evergreen needle. It had obviously come from our beautiful Christmas tree which is called a Chrismon tree. It had stood near the altar a couple of months ago and now was packed away in storage. It had been beautifully decorated with only ornaments that represented the life story of Christ: angels, crosses, butterflies representing the resurrection and ascension, the Bible, the chalice from the Last Supper, the fisherman's sandals of Christ, and numerous others.

The vivid image of this glorious tree with its white ornaments trimmed in gold and silver highlighting my Savior's story came rushing back to me. My recalling this in the midst of receiving the sacraments was a synchronized moment from the Holy Spirit. Communion cannot be celebrated without the Christmas story, and I was reminded of my Savior's life as it was represented on the Chrismon tree. I was now commemorating all that He had given to provide me a seat at His table. I bowed in gratitude as I recalled His Words to His disciples in *Luke 22":19 "Do this to remember me."*

Our Father is constantly asking us to remember Him and who He is. Throughout the ages, He has inspired people to share His thrilling message of life eternal in ways that cause others to see Him in their hearts. Throughout human history God has given visual evidence of His presence in the lives of His people just as Jesus did with His disciples the night before He died.

God has continued to implant these images in the spirits of His people today. The inspiration of creating symbols that represent the life of Jesus and placing them on an evergreen Christmas tree began in 1940 with George Pass, a pastor of a Lutheran Church in Danville, Virginia. He was inspired to help his congregation receive the blessing of seeing the story of Christ when they looked at the Christmas tree in their church sanctuary, not just a decorated tree. The Holy Spirit certainly must have guided this man of God as he searched for a way to construct these vivid reminders of the life and ministry of Jesus.

Pastor Pass lived during a frugal time in our country when

most people saved and repurposed things, and so he used left-over scraps of Christmas wrapping paper and trimmings to craft his distinctive ornaments. My Grandmother Overstreet and many of her generation practiced this kind of creativity out of necessity. They knew how to make toys out of socks and dolls out of clothes pins and paper. They loved using their hands to express what was in their hearts. I wish I could go back in time and watch Pastor Pass make his simple decorations as the fire of inspiration stirred within him. This was the Holy Spirit at work!

The story that began with this pastor continued in 1957, when a woman named Frances Kipps Spencer continued the idea of making Christmas tree ornaments that told the story of Jesus. She introduced a new kind of Christmas tree to her church which she decided to call a Chrismon tree. It was decorated with just Christian monograms which are a combination of letters to form an abbreviation for the name of Jesus Christ. Later, she was inspired to make a change in her Chrismon decorations. She wanted them to be more personal so that they represented the life of Jesus. Her designs then began to make God's Word come alive as they highlighted the ministry, activities, nature and teachings of Christ.

Just as the Holy Spirit was at work in Pastor Pass's efforts, He was directing the work of Ms. Spencer. I love it that her name was Spencer, because even though I know of no family connection with her, my maiden name was Spencer. Maybe she was related to me, or maybe she could have even been a member of your own family from long ago. Still, many of us have "inherited" her desire to tell the story of Jesus however we can.

What she did to make Christmas tree ornaments memorable has struck a resonant chord with people across our country for over the past sixty years. Eventually her story unfolded in such a way that kits of her designs are made and offered for purchase. The hands of thousands of people now replicate what Ms. Spencer accomplished. These people are like the craftsmen of King Solomon's temple when they make things with their own hands that glorify God. The simple designs utilize beautiful materials of gold, silver, and pearls which makes them appealing for any house of worship.

During the Christmas season, Chrismon trees in churches across our nation now hold memory stones to highlight the life of our Lord. Each design portrays some truth about God as seen in Jesus, and in so doing, the Word of God is being shared. The message is there if people can look for it with spiritual eyes instead of worldly eyes. That was the purpose which originated with a church pastor all those years ago.

For almost fifty years our church has been a part of this continuing story by placing a tree of Christian symbols in our sanctuary. About ten years ago two members, Sue Stone and Kae Brown, realized the first set of ornaments was getting worn out. To continue presenting our tree as a worthy offering of praise and worship of our Lord, they decided there needed to be a church-wide project to make new decorations.

This project was greeted with enthusiasm by our congregation. Countless hours were spent raising money to purchase Chrismon kits* and then more than sixty men, women and children of our church assembled over 300 of these beautiful ornaments. Many were created in memory of loved ones or in honor of family members. All the dedications were recorded in a booklet by Sue and Kae so they could be recognized by our congregation and known by worshippers who would come in the future. All the "craftsmen" of our church were providing beautiful memory stones for our Chrismon tree, just as those who had done almost fifty years ago. The story would continue.

These fascinating pieces feature a variety of different designs. Every one of them delivers an individual message from Scripture that communicates how treasured we are by the living God. Each Christmas our congregation looks expectantly for the appearance of the Chrismon tree, to again see all of the memory stones that are placed on it. Every year this sight brings a refreshing announcement of the birth of our Lord! It makes the message new again for us, and makes our joy of receiving it abundant!

Evergreen trees like the one we use for our Chrismon tree represents Christ Himself, and are a perfect place to feature symbols about His life. The evergreen tree is also a reminder of human salvation and forgiveness through Jesus. That is why Peter wrote, *"He himself bore our sins in his body on the tree, that we might die to sin and live to righteousness. By his wounds you have been healed."(1 Peter 2:24.)*

Even the needle-like leaves of the evergreen tree pointing upwards gives an inspiring message. They remind us that the destiny of human beings is to reach God in heaven, fostered by the water of His love. Their withstanding the severe winter and still remaining green encourages us to remember faith in God can withstand any temptation or trial and keep the soul evergreen. An evergreen soul—we all want that to carry us through our days on this earth!

The late Pope John Paul said in Christmas of 2004, "The Christmas tree is an ancient custom that exalts the value of life, because the evergreen tree remains unchanged through the harshness of winter. When gifts are arranged under the tree, it becomes a symbol of the 'tree of life,' a figure of Christ, God's greatest gift to man."

When we decorate trees in our homes, many of us retrieve boxes of ornaments from our closets and attics. Sometimes, when we remove the ornaments, we rediscover the sentimental attachment we have for them. I know that in those moments, I have a quiet joy as I touch each one. Do you experience that also?

Some of our decorations may be hand-made by our children or grandchildren, associated with seasons in our lives, or may have originally belonged to someone who is no longer with us. Does the living God have moments of joyful sentiment when He sees us retrieving those that represent something about His Son's life? Does He smile when He sees us carefully put them in a place of honor on our trees, and then go into His house of worship to sing songs of celebration about the birth of His Son? Perhaps, as *Zephaniah* said in *Chapter 3, verse 17, He sings with us.*

*kits can be purchased through Rufty's Christian Symbol Kits, 280 Furniture Drive, Salisbury, NC 28146

Every Christmas season most of us take for granted the message of hope that was given to the world over two thousand years ago. Reading in the Old Testament, we can see that for hundreds of years God's people yearned and ached for the promised Messiah to come into the world. King David gave prophecy of Jesus, the prophet Isaiah spoke fervently of Him, and yet the world turned and turned without His appearance.

Three wise men had watched for every possible sign of the long expected Savior to the world. They were so ready for this miracle that when they identified the blazing star in the sky, they were convinced God had given them a sign, and they started out on a very long journey to find Him. They found Him because they had waited expectantly for Him!

The world will say that my finding that evergreen needle in February and subsequently taking you down this memory lane was just a coincidence. Some will also say my mind made too much of a needle that had somehow been missed by a vacuum cleaner. However, the more I seek the Lord and look for Him, the more of these synchronized inspirations I experience.

God is giving us messages of His enduring presence everywhere we look. All that we experience with Him can be memory stones of our receiving the greatest gift ever given to the world- The King of Kings, The Lord of Lords, The Messiah, Immanuel, and our Savior! Tell His story to the world! Isn't He thrilling! Celebrate Him!

The Chrismon tree in
our church's sanctuary,
2017

It is the first of January
(2016) and time to
take down the tree,
but Easter is coming!
Thank you, Father!

Exodus 35:20-21

So the whole community of Israel left Moses, and returned to their tents. All whose hearts were stirred and whose spirits were moved came and brought their sacred offerings to the LORD. They brought all the materials needed for the Tabernacle, for the performance of its rituals, and for the sacred garments.

Chapter Fifteen

Memory Stones from Ghana, Africa

Memory stones are sometimes made of cloth

Who buys twenty-four hundred yards of cloth to commemorate what the Lord has done for them? The Christ the King Ghana Methodist Church* which resides in a small town, Winder, Georgia, has a huge heart for our Lord and a need to worship Him with all their strength, minds, and spirits. They also made the purchase of all this cloth!

They recognized that their community of worshippers who first resided in Ghana, but has now been transported by the living God to the United States of America, had been blessed every step of their journey by Him! This congregation decided to commemorate its five year anniversary with a visual image that represented the victories they had experienced in their faith walk with the Lord. The story of this fabric reaching their hands is a wonderful memory stone for you and me.

Their church was organized as a Ghana Methodist Church so that members who had come to our country from Ghana could worship in their own language and in their own unique

131

way as it is practiced in their homeland. Perfect English is intertwined with the melodic language of their home country. They speak with a delightful British accent because of the history of Ghana being ruled by Britain almost a hundred years before its independence in 1957.

Having time to worship together enables the Ghanaians to know about each other's needs and to be able to offer each other assistance in times of difficulty. This closeness facilitates the celebrating of their culture, but at the same time makes them powerful through strength given to them by the Lord to bless the country in which they reside. They have a great love for our country as well as each other and the family members who still live in Ghana!

Their worship services are lively and joy filled! They even dance when they take up their offering to the Lord. They spend several minutes singing and dancing around colorful buckets that represent each day of the week. They put their offering in the one that represents the day of the week on which they were born. Do you know the day of the week on which you were born? You better Google this before you go visit their church, and then you will have a lot of fun giving your offering. King David would have loved worshipping with them! I can just see him dancing as the offering is given.

They sing traditional hymns, and they sing them enthusiastically with boisterous voices and arms in the air. Nothing in their worship services is done in a half-hearted manner! What about prayers in their services? They pray loudly and forcefully for Ghana, the United States, for personal matters, for healing, and every concern that the Lord has laid on their hearts. They lift up their voices in a mighty way, believing their prayers are being sent right into the throne room of the living God. I can tell you, if you have a prayer concern, you definitely want them to pray for you!

I know all of this first hand, because I have a few family members who are worshippers in this small, but mighty and

powerful church the Lord has touched. I have been extremely blessed on occasion to worship with them. I claim Joseph,
Karen, and their young son whose name is also Joseph, as my
children. They are not the children of my blood, but of my
heart. Many years ago, I asked our Lord to send us a wonderful
Christian man "who was on fire for Him" to bless our family.
He went all the way to Ghana and chose Joseph to answer my
prayer! I received a bonus answer to my request when Joseph
came with his wife and young son.

Who is Joseph from Ghana? When he first came here
many years ago, my friend Gloria asked him to speak to her
small, "spirit-filled" church. Joseph doesn't do anything half
way, and he gave a testimony that revealed the victory in the
Lord he experiences every day. This humble man is confident
in whom he knows as his Heavenly Father, and he fervently
seeks for others to also know Him.

Later, Gloria shared with me what she saw when he was
speaking to the congregation of her church. "Joseph was
surrounded by uneven edges of light like prisms. It was so
blinding, I could hardly focus on his words!" Joseph once
laughed and said to me, "Your country used to send mission-
aries to Ghana, and now our country sends them to you!" It is
obvious to everyone who meets him that he is anointed by the
Lord to bless our country.

The United States of America is certainly in dire need of
spiritual blessings and we are so fortunate to receive them
from Joseph and his family. They have come at a great sacrifice. They have three daughters in Ghana who have not been
able to join them. They have been here for several years, sharing Jesus with everyone they meet. Joseph and Karen were
both accomplished lawyers in their homeland, but have taken
low-paying jobs here to support themselves. They have sought
to model serving others in our country as our Lord did when
He walked this earth. My prayer is that God will bless them by
granting all the desires of their hearts, and that includes their

daughters being able to join them.

Once their church decided to design and order commemorative cloth for their five year anniversary, there were many obstacles placed in front of them. Their experience is reminiscent of God choosing to have the nation of Israel cross the Jordan River when it was at flood stage. He wanted His people to know by whose power they were able to cross!

By the time the cloth reached the faithful Ghanaians, everyone in the congregation knew it was sacred clothing they would wear, and that it came to them by the hand of God. What they accomplished had not been done by any Ghana church in the United States or in Canada. This achievement is even more impressive when you realize they are a very small church of about fifty members, while many of the Ghana Churches here have hundreds of people in their congregations. All of this makes me believe that God loved weaving together a modern day "David and Goliath" story with the journey of their twenty-four hundred yards of fabric!

The mission of this extraordinary church to glorify God reminded them of the one facing the people of Israel after they had crossed the Jordan River at flood stage thousands of years ago. They desired to honor God in the same way as Joshua and the twelve men, one from each tribe, honored God when they placed memorial stones in their camp and the Jordan River. The people of Israel saw the stones and remembered, and when every succeeding generation asked about the stones, the story of the power of God was repeated.

The Ghanaians prayed that people seeing their garments of praise would recognize their uniqueness and be curious enough to ask questions. These questions would open the door for them to tell others about our living God.

The first step in their quest was to create a design for the cloth that represented their testimony for the Lord. It was very personal to them, and they wanted it to reflect what He had done in their lives here in the United States. This design could not possibly be found on any fabric that had already been made, and the only place that could produce this special cloth was a textile factory in Ghana.

God continued paving the path for them when Karen and Joseph's daughter, who is also named Karen, found favor with a fellow college student in Ghana. He had been studying pharmacy but also had a hobby as an artist. He drew the design according to the directions given by Karen's parents, knowing that every image was to glorify God!

This young college student obviously had been chosen by the Lord to put heart-felt testimony onto a design that could be imprinted on cloth. Though the process of communication for the design could not be done in person, technology provided a successful way for it to happen. Texting, emails, and other methods of communicating have never been put to better use. God can use anything including technology for His glory!

It was decided that everything about the cloth needed to reflect light, and so candles were chosen to be prominently displayed in the background. Green was chosen as a background color to highlight the message of light, and several large red crosses were added with the words under them: "A light Unto the Nations." The words "Christ the King" were written in English and also the words: "Christ ntsi, Yeye Adehye" from their native language in Ghana. These words are translated "Christ the King Royal." They wanted it known that because Christ is royal, we as his children, are also royal!

The design was then given to someone who works with textile design, and this person then presented it to a textile factory that makes cloth. Another hurdle was then presented. This factory did not print special, individualized cloth for any amounts less than five thousand yards! However, the lady chosen by the Lord to present this request had great favor with the people at the factory, and they relented to make just half that amount, twenty- four hundred yards! God was granting favor to this small Ghana church every step of the way!

Another obstacle was the cost. To manufacture the fabric would cost a few thousand dollars, which this small congregation did not have! A person of God's choosing whose name was Sis Juliana BenEghan, stepped forward to receive the order and paid for it in full. She had faith that God would reimburse her for the expense. Thank you, Juliana. I have not met you, but I love you!

Karen's supportive parents, Nana and Mrs. Kofi Nsaful allocated space in their home to store this massive amount of cloth. What wonderful, God fearing people they are! I am sure God is proud of their efforts, and I pray that He rewards them for their faithfulness. The fabric then came to the United States in stages as people visited their homeland and then returned with large bolts of it. Gradually, the cloth was paid for and the woman of faith who had stepped forward to pay was given what she was owed. God did that. Isn't He wonderful!

When the congregation had received its first five hundred yards of cloth, they had a special worship service to ask the Lord to bless it. Anointing oil was poured on a section of the cloth, and then all of it was saturated with the prayers of thankful hearts of the people. It had arrived on a journey of faith and would proceed only with the hand of the Lord guiding it the rest of the way.

Joseph and Karen are, as they say in Ghana, "Local Preachers" for their church. As leaders of their church, they ensured that everything concerning the cloth's transformation into clothing was pleasing to the Lord. Christians in their country have very unique ideas about clothing worn for worship, and what is worn for worship, cannot be worn for work or play.

The anointed cloth which they took and had made into clothing for the entire congregation is especially considered to be sacred. They desire above all else that their garments look priestly, not worldly, and be honorable to the Lord in all ways. They have a fervent desire that their love and reverence for the living God be reflected by their choice of clothing for worship!

Their testimony for God has not gone unnoticed by those of distinction in The Ghana Methodist Church back home in Ghana. The Most Reverend Titus Awotwi Pratt who has the high office of Presiding Bishop of The Methodist Church Ghana was recently visiting the States. He had a detailed itinerary which did not include visiting a small town in the state of Georgia.

Somehow, when he was in Atlanta, he heard about this small church and asked Karen and Joseph to come meet with him. After his time with them, he decided to detour from the beaten path. He felt inspired to come see for himself what was so special about this little church in a small town. A couple of days before his departure back to Ghana, he left a Sunday service early in order to visit their church that evening. That was extremely rare for the Bishop to do! I just love it when the Holy Spirit whispers in our ears and changes our preconceived plans! He was telling the Bishop that He had something He wanted him to see!

The entire church was thrilled with his visit, and recognized that this kind of favor could only come from God, Himself. The congregation wore their garments of praise that had come all the way from Ghana, and then were sewn by loving hands in the United States. The Bishop reported to Joseph and Karen, "The spiritual temperature in your church is very high, and you should continue to spread the Gospel here in the United States." Our country is very, very blessed to have this congregation of Ghanaians in our country!

*Christ the King Ghana Methodist Church
208C North Broad Street
Winder, GA 30680

Why go to this much difficulty to produce a garment of praise for our God to reveal what He has done? I am sure God smiled on this congregation, seeing their desire for their adoration for Him to be recognized by others as they worshipped! From the moment the idea was conceived to make a memory stone of cloth to commemorate the miracles God had created in their lives, God was at work. He allowed this small congregation to do what had not been done before in even churches much larger than theirs. He made them mighty for the glory of His name. He gave them "eagle's wings." He can also give them to you.

It's not the hundreds of yards of cloth that has any significance. It is the hearts that brought it to our country. This small Ghana church could see God's Hand every step of the way. What impossible dream do you have to glorify God? Has He asked you to step out in faith? Remember what He has done for others when the impossible was made possible. God's Word has thousands of these stories.

God's anointed ones will someday be given white robes of righteousness. I can't wait to put on my robe! Today, whatever you wear when you worship, let it be a garment of joy and praise for God. Worship Him with all that is in you! He is so worthy! Let His countenance shine upon you, so that others will see Him in you!

L to R: Jeff & Julie Cornelius, the Most Reverend Titus Awotwi Pratt, Karen & Joseph Essiful-Ansah

It was such an honor to meet The Most Reverend Titus Awotwi Pratt!

The congregation of Christ the King Ghana Methodist Church

Psalm 19:1-4

The heavens proclaim the glory of God. The skies display his craftsmanship. Day after day they continue to speak; night after night they make him known. They speak without a sound or word; their voice is never heard. Yet their message has gone throughout the earth, and their words to all the world.

Psalm 148:1-6*

Praise the LORD! Praise the LORD from the heavens! Praise him from the skies! Praise him, all his angels! Praise him, all the armies of heaven! Praise him, sun, and moon! Praise him, all you twinkling stars! Praise him, skies above! Praise him, vapors high above the clouds! Let every created thing give praise to the LORD, for he issued his command, and they came into being; He set them in place forever and ever. His decree will never be revoked.

Chapter Sixteen

Musical Memory Stones Orchestrated by the living God

All creation sings God's praise

"*Heaven and earth* are full of Your glory!" These are words our church choir sang recently during our worship service as our spirit-filled choir director led us and threw his head back in pure delight of the Lord. I love the moments of exhilaration we all experience as we sing to our Lord. Our director had inspired us when he spoke about his trip to Yellowstone National Park just the week before, where he saw so many exciting and beautiful scenes that revealed the glory of the Lord. He gently asked us to remember our own moments of ecstasy with the Lord, as we sang the words to our song.

I have a truly magnificent time every Sunday when I stand with our small church choir and sing praises to God. Our Heavenly Father is so thrilling, and I love to sing to Him! I really enjoy singing the old hymns which are some of the most amazing testimony I have ever read. This genre of music has fallen out of favor for many worshippers today, and I used to be one of those who didn't appreciate singing many of the hymns. I struggled with words that seemed so formal and difficult to sing.

Today, the lyrics just jump off the page for me. My relationship with these old hymns began to change when I started reading the historical background of some of them. I also purchased two volumes of a book written by Robert J. Morgan which are entitled "Then Sings My Soul." If you read the stories in his books, you will weep at what he recorded about some of the people who wrote many of the old hymns which are in our worship books. One of them speaks about Horatio G. Spafford writing lyrics to the song, "It Is Well with My Soul," after losing his only son to scarlet fever and then later his three daughters at sea. His wife and daughters were aboard the luxurious French liner *Ville du Havre*, on their way to Europe for a vacation when it collided with an iron sailing vessel and sank. Only his wife survived. How could he write such inspirational words in the midst of overwhelming grief? The Holy Spirit surely led him as he wrote such a moving testimony. Remarkably, there are hundreds of moving stories like Mr. Spafford's demonstrating the work of the Holy Spirit when many of our stirring hymns were created.

By the Hand of God through this kind of music, some of the most inspirational memory stones ever were given to the world. The lyrics reveal a faith that is supernatural and upholds God's people in times that challenge the very fiber of their being. Much of our traditional music is based on Scripture and becomes very powerful testimony when it is sung. Many of the Psalms in the Old Testament written by King David were meant to be a praise offering of song to our God. It's all about our hearts when we sing to Him, and singing from His Word is singing in His language.

I like all kinds of music and enjoy the spirit of contemporary Christian music. So many of the songs have lyrics that make you want to move, lift your hands, and sing from the top of your voice. I really enjoy participating when I am in a large group and don't have to worry about sometimes singing off key! I have been known to do that on occasion. I can carry a tune and read music, but sometimes I accidentally make up my own notes! Other times, I take pleasure in being in a small, loving church choir. I honestly believe God placed me there so I could experience the gift of fellowship with Him and the other choir members. His sense of humor may have also been at work! (For years I told people I could not sing, and the first time I appeared in the choir loft, some of my friends almost slid out of their pews laughing. I laughed good-naturally with them, and I am sure God laughed with all of us!)

I love Michael W. Smith's song "The Heart of Worship" which talks about soul- searching that brings a worshipper's heart back to God and speaks to the knowing that it's all about Him. The lyrics also speak about the need to sing with every breath you take in a way that will bless God's heart. Bless God's heart—I want to do that by singing heartfelt words! Michael W. Smith, I am with you all the way when you sing about worship that blesses God! So much of today's contemporary Christian music speaks to me in a powerful way, as if I were having a special prayer time with my Lord. It is so refreshing! I have Vicki Yohe's recording of "Anoint Me Lord" and in this song she asks the Lord to fill her with His anointing oil as she goes about her day. Asking the Lord to be filled with His anointing oil is also my prayer for every day of my life.

We have had gifted musicians and beautiful worship music for thousands of years. King David knew the importance of music in worshipping God, and made sure accomplished musicians participated. *1 Chronicles 25:6-8* speaks about how they were organized under his direction. There were those playing cymbals, stringed instruments, and harps, and there was no regard for whether they were young or old, teacher or student! He sought out people who had a heart for God which was reflected in their spirits when they worshipped. They were not just going through the motions of celebrating God. King David knew about the heart of worship a few thousand years before Michael W. Smith wrote his song.

Many times as I prepare for worship in our church, I ask God to send His angels to sing with us. I believe that praise music, whether it is traditional or contemporary, is lifted right into God's throne room where millions of angels are singing continuous praise to our Lord. Our voices join with theirs. I also believe when we start singing God's praises His angels join with ours.

One Sunday after our choir sang the powerful anthem "Only God" by Mary McDonald, someone in the congregation remarked, "It was as if there were many more voices being heard than there were people singing!" I believe those extra voices are there every Sunday when we lift up our songs of praise. On this particular Sunday, God allowed them to be heard. Much of Scripture reveals we were born to worship Him. God's Word tells us in *Isaiah 42:10* , "*Sing a new song to the LORD! Sing his praises from the ends of the earth!*" When we do this, God is magnified and we experience His favor in a mighty way.

Our songs of worship are a blessing to us and our God, but He does not depend on *just* our songs to receive worship. We have no idea about the expanse of the worship which is continuously surrounding the throne of God. Besides the millions of angels present, there is a symphony of sounds made by the universe that is bigger than our wildest dreams.

God has allowed the people on earth today to be blessed through unbelievable advances in technology (which He Himself created) and to be given tremendous knowledge about our solar system, our galaxy, and the whole universe. Scripture tells us that the whole universe sings praises to God. Is Scripture just being poetic? Looking at the body of science that has been revealed to us today gives us a thrilling answer.

Our Earth is just one of the planets that circle our sun, and

146

our sun is just one of more than 200 billion stars in the Milky Way galaxy. Our galaxy is one of billions of galaxies across the vast expanse of the cosmos. Everything in the universe is in constant motion and making sounds, but human ears simply cannot detect much of what is being created. God, however, hears all of His creation speaking and singing to Him.

Scientists tell us that sound is created when matter vibrates, and is heard when it has a medium to travel through. Our vocal sounds are made when air moves over our vocal chords and are heard when these sounds vibrate through air. What about when there is nothing to carry the sound? Outer space is a virtual vacuum—does that mean that no sound exists there? God must smile when we say there are no sounds being made in outer space. Read the book of Job in the Old Testament and consider the conversation God has with Job about the creation of the universe. Job had much to learn about the power and might of our living God and so do we!

Scientists also tell us that all matter vibrates and has a resonant frequency—it all makes sound waves! Throughout the universe there is movement and these vibrations produce sounds that we simply can't hear. If we could hear them, we would hear the entire universe singing to God!

Astrophysicist William Chaplin gives us an inspiring glimpse into the continuous celestial symphony serenading God. He says that the smallest stars are flutes, the medium-sized ones are trombones, and the giant stars are reverberating tubas. How do they do that? They have internal vibrations which cause their subtle, rhythmic brightening and dimming. The turbulent rise and fall of hot gases on the star's surface penetrates deep into its interior and this produces resonating tones. Each star in the universe emits its own distinct sound, and if we could listen to them in groups, we would hear musical sounds. We can't hear them, but God can!

Louie Giglio knows about musical sounds created from stars. He is a gifted pastor of a church in Atlanta, Georgia, and author of the book *The Air I Breathe: Worship as a Way of Life*.* He recently demonstrated the phenomena of celestial music in a video. He convincingly said that God, through His creation, creates music that pleases Him and inspires his children. In his video he used sounds retrieved by NASA's specially designed equipment like space probes and the Nasa Voyager. He combined the captured sound of vibrating pulsars which are thousands of light years away, sounds of singing whales, and a recording of "How Great Is Our God" to demonstrate how the universe is singing to God.

Watching Pastor Giglio lead a church congregation in worship as they listened to some of these combined sounds gave me a breathtaking insight to all the worship that is taking place all over the universe. I want to be a part of that. I want to be a part of God's symphony! Don't you?

There is exhilarating music resonating in the universe every day. In the movie "August Rush" the lead character is a little boy who hears music all around him. He hears it in street noises, wind rushing through a field, in the rhythm of tools being used in a street, and in everything around him. Do you hear music all around you?

Do you hear the music that exists in others? Do you hear it in your heart when you worship God? The music that God is listening to is not coming from your mouth. It is coming from your heart. The entire universe is singing to God! Let's hold up our part in God's symphony. Let's join in with others, with the singing whales, with all the creatures on the earth, the stars, the planets and the entire universe and bring forth sounds that God hears as praise. Make musical memory stones that bless the very heart of God and "infect" everyone around you with joy!

*The Air I breathe: Worship as a Way of Life, 2003, Multnomah Books: A division of Random House, Inc.

So here I am in the place of worship, eyes open, drinking in your strength and glory. In your generous love I am really living at last! My lips brim praises like fountains. I bless you every time I take a breath; my arms wave like banners of praise to you.

Psalm 63:2-5 * The Message

† Barbara J. Cornelius †

Revelation 19:6-9*

The Marriage Supper of the Lamb
Then I heard what seemed to be the voice of a great multitude, like the roar of many waters and like the sound of mighty peals of thunder, crying out, "Hallelujah! For the Lord our God the Almighty reigns.

"Let us rejoice and exult and give him the glory, for the marriage of the Lamb has come, and his Bride has made herself ready; it was granted her to clothe herself with fine linen, bright and pure"—for the fine linen is righteous deed of the saints.

And the angel said to me, "Write this: Blessed are those who are invited to the marriage supper of the Lamb ." And he said to me, "These are the true words of God."

*English Standard Version

Chapter Seventeen

A Wedding Dress Full of Memory Stones

There is no time limit on celebrating God's memory stones

One of my most treasured memory stones hangs on a decorative folding screen in my prayer room. It reminds me of what a blessed life I have had every time I look at it. Gratitude swells up inside of me every time I see my half century wedding gown which rests on a hanger made of decorative pearls. I have pinned sentimental keepsake pictures on this dress. They are from my husband's and mine wedding, as well as from our son's and daughter's weddings. These pictures remind me of fervently prayed requests to God for my own happiness and for the happiness of my children. When I look at the evidence of some of the many blessings I have received over a long life, I wonder, "Where has time gone? Can it actu-

153

ally have been that many years since I purchased this dress?"

Actually, I am grateful for every year. I am very pleased to have two adult children and eight grandchildren who give me excuses to play again. I am drenched in prosperity from the Lord. A few years ago, I decided to fetch my wedding dress from the back of a closet. This cherished gown was originally a light ivory color and is now a very antique yellow. I was very pleased to retrieve it from the closet and use it for a special kind of "bulletin board" for pictures that give a constant reminder of answered prayers for my family. I smile every time I see my wedding dress.

Our son, Jeff, and his wife Julie were married on my husband's and my thirty-ninth wedding anniversary. Six months later our daughter and her husband were married with her five-year-old daughter and seven-year-old son from her first marriage as their attendants. My daughter-in-law and son-in-law are truly gifts from God. Larry and I are so blessed to have them in our family. They are not our biological children, but they are definitely the children of our hearts.

It doesn't seem possible that it has been over fifty years since I purchased my wedding dress during my senior year at Indiana, University. A friend and I had walked downtown from our dorm to a store in Bloomington, Indiana just to see what was available. My eyes went straight to the rack of wedding dresses marked fifty percent off. I fell in love with a long ivory dress that was accented with tiny pearls on a scooped neckline and large pieces of antique looking lace on the skirt. When I saw that it fit perfectly, I promptly gave the clerk a check for fifty dollars. This was my best impulse buy of all time. I was thrilled to get the dress of my dreams for such a good price. The endorphins were flowing!

My friend and I then went to lunch with the wedding dress in tow. (Yes, I took my wedding dress which was in a large box into the restaurant!) We were way too giddy all through lunch, and could barely eat! We left and had gone a short distance down the street when we heard the voice of our waitress! She had chased us out the door to remind us we had not paid our bill. I hate to think how that could have turned out, but the favor of the Lord was upon us, and she smiled when I told her about being overly excited after purchasing my wedding gown.

I don't remember too much about the wedding ceremony which happened on December 18, 1965, but I do know it was one of the happiest days of my life! I was floating on a cloud of joy the entire time. Some of those who attended Larry's and my wedding talked about how I cried, and others talked about how happy I seemed. Both observations were accurate, but believe me the tears were those of happiness.

I still have a few of our wedding gifts and am stunned that two in particular have survived my clumsy hands—two antique candy dishes my high school art teacher gave me. One is a sky blue color and the other is a very light green. Both are somewhat delicate but have been used numerous times over the years for family celebrations. Mrs. Bott would be so proud to see they are still intact!

The very best remaining wedding gift is a large white King James Bible my parents gave us. I have to admit it was more of a decorative item for many, many years before the contents were treasured. Giving the Word of God to newlyweds and praying His Word for their lives is the very best gift you can give them. This is the kind of deposit in their world that many times will not reap immediate, visible rewards, but God hears every prayer and not one syllable is wasted. Spend lavishly with your prayers for those you love when they begin the journey of marriage.

The very best enduring evidence of our wedding is not anything that can be purchased—it is that Larry Cornelius is still with me! He has never been bored. Frustrated, yes, but not bored! We don't love every moment we have had in our marriage, but we treasure every day and every year we have been given. I am so thankful the Lord gave us each other and directed our path, so we could not only grow old together, but most importantly, grow spiritually towards Him.

Recently, I found our wedding book listing all our guests, gifts, wedding announcement, cards and other memories of that big day in our lives which was only a week before Christmas. Between two of the pages, a card tumbled out from the Christmas Larry and I celebrated our first year anniversary. The card was from a childhood friend, Ann, who was with me from first grade through our college years. I absolutely adored Ann!

I spent several nights at her house during our childhood. I survived several of those sleep-overs with her huge Alaskan Husky getting into bed with us and also sitting unquietly next to our chairs at the dinner table! That dog barked intermittently for food to come his way, and scared the fool out of me. I loved Ann too much to complain. Besides, he was part of the deal to have her as a friend, and it was a wonderful bargain!

Ann and her husband were married four months before Larry and I were married. I spent time with them in their apartment, which was not too far from my dorm on campus. I enjoyed having meals with them and laughing about their recent adventures as newlyweds. They were so in love, and I was very supportive of a young man who cherished my friend. I still remember her showing me some of her favorite wedding gifts, including pewter cups that she said would last forever.

Inside Ann's Christmas card from all those years ago was an aged, long-forgotten newspaper clipping I had stored away. It was Ann and her husband's wedding announcement, and it pictured her radiating with joy in her wedding dress. Oh, what an absolute, beautiful smiling face was seen in this long ago picture.

Ann's smile was contagious, and she always made me smile back. She had that effect on people, and her humor, which was not always appreciated by some of our teachers in middle school and high school, was a delight to me. That girl was funny! Her smiling face in this yellowed photo reminded me of that. Remembrance of all that happiness washed over me.

When Ann sent the card, she and Don had also celebrated their first year anniversary and were looking forward to celebrating Christmas with family a few hundred miles away. Ann spoke about how busy their lives were, and she described how graduate school and work activities were consuming their waking moments.

Ann and Don were killed a few days after I received her card. Their car slid off a slick, snow-covered road. There was no other vehicle involved in their accident, and it was believed that Don may have fallen asleep at the wheel. He had worked all night, and without his having slept at all, they then headed out on their long trip. They were only about one hour from home when their car went off the road and overturned. They were killed instantly. Their funeral was two days after Christmas on December 27th. Sharing those words with you still stings my heart.

I hadn't seen the card and Ann's wedding picture for many, many years. I didn't need to. I have carried my friend's heart with me all these long years that I have been gifted to live. I too was in an accident the same year as Don and Ann's. I could well have died, but I didn't. I do not know why their story was finished, but mine was continued. I do know that I am eternally grateful for the years given to me, and I will see Don and Ann again in heaven.

Writing about my aged wedding dress, and seeing Ann's wedding dress in a newspaper clipping reminded me again of the two starkly different stories that followed the wedding pictures. Tragedy followed one, and a long marriage followed another. I can't even ask God "why?" I know I trust Him because all of my life He has revealed Himself to me in ways that show me how to trust Him. His Word gives this security to me.

Six years after Ann left this earth my husband and I remembered her in a way that has blessed us for over forty years. We named our daughter Jennifer after my friend Ann. We gave her Ann's name for her middle name. Our beautiful daughter carrying her name has been a wonderful memory for me all these years. I would say that I wish Ann knew about Jennifer Ann, but honestly I think she knew about her before Larry and I did. I still grieve for Ann and her husband Don, but I believe with every fiber of my being that the best is yet to come, and they just got a head start!

My wedding dress had another outing several years before our fiftieth wedding anniversary party. It was used for a "wedding reception" in a DVD Bible Study on Revelation which was presented by a well-known Christian author and speaker, Beth Moore. All of us in our group were inspired by Beth's teaching and God's Word in Chapter nineteen of the book of Revelation. This chapter described the marriage supper with the Lamb of God, and in *Matthew 25:1-13* we reveled in Christ Himself comparing the coming of His kingdom to a wedding for which all of us must be prepared.

We had a glorious time that evening. My wedding dress was on display with memorabilia and pictures that several of the ladies had brought from their own weddings. We had refreshments which even included an actual wedding cake. We took pictures of the evening and made a photo album to share with others, so we could tell them about the wedding feast that awaits all of God's children. We were delirious with the excitement of this promise for the future! We still are.

Look at the promise of hope and love you see when a wedding comes into your life experience. No matter what the outcome is for these earthly celebrations, we have a promise from the living God that the future which awaits us with Him, will be the most glorious ever experienced.

Not only is the best yet to come, be convinced that it is the best that ever existed in the entire universe! Stay in God's Word to get all the glorious details. Jesus, we cannot wait until you come again and call forth your kingdom for all of eternity!

Here's the wedding dress before it became a "bulletin board."
Larry's and my wedding day, December 18, 1965.

MARRIED IN BOWLING GREEN — Mrs. Don Glenn Tillotson was before her marriage Miss Ann Butler, daughter of Mr. and Mrs. Lochel Butler, Brazil. Mr. Tillotson is the son of Mr. and Mrs. Don C. Tillotson, Fulton, Ill. The couple now lives in Bloomington.   Portrait by Lawrence-Krehe.

My friend, Ann Butler Tillotson—I still love you!

John 11: 40-44

So they rolled the stone aside. Then Jesus looked up to heaven and said, "Father, thank you for hearing me. You always hear me, but I said it out loud for the sake of all these people standing there, so they will believe you sent me." Then Jesus shouted, "Lazarus, come out!" And Lazarus came out, bound in grave clothes, his face wrapped in a head cloth. Jesus told them, "Unwrap him and let him go!"

Revelation 21: 5

And the one sitting on the throne said, "Look, I am making everything new!"

Isaiah 61:10

I am overwhelmed with joy in the LORD my God! For he has dressed me with the clothing of salvation and draped me in a robe of righteousness. I am like a bridegroom in his wedding suit or a bride with her jewels.

Chapter Eighteen

Memory Stones from Eternity

Memory stones are not limited by our time on earth

"*Now for the* rest of the story!" Those were the familiar words of famous radio personality Paul Harvey. For over fifty years this devoted Christian man was the most listened-to radio personality in America. He reached twenty four million people a week on over twelve hundred radio stations. He captivated his listeners in five minute story segments which recounted true historical events laced with intriguing mystery. Just when he had captured your attention, he would say, "I will be back after commercial break for the rest of the story!" Upon returning to the air, he would then reveal some surprising twist to the story that left his audience in amazement.

He told some of the most incredible stories about the famous and the infamous, the courageous and the unknown. Some of the titles of his stories were: "The Stammering Secret Agent Who Changed the Course of History," "The Incredible Survivor of the Battle of Little Big Horn," "The Goat Who Has Kept the Cubs from Winning a Pennant Since 1945," and hundreds others. Many of these stories were recorded in four of Paul Harvey's best-selling books which are now a treasured part of my personal library. Paul Harvey died in 2009 at the age of ninety and is greatly missed by millions of people, including me.

Paul Harvey would have appreciated knowing about a remarkable letter I received a few years ago from a World War Two veteran, Fred A. Overton. He had written a short note under the return address: "I have visited Lazarus's second burial location. See inside." He had seen where the local newspaper had published an article about a book signing I had done for my first book *Lazarus Still Rises*. It seemed that he wanted to provide his own "the rest of the story" like Paul Harvey had done so successfully for many years. Perhaps the title would have been *Lazarus's Life after Death*.

Inside the envelope was a newspaper article he had written about an extraordinary experience he had during World War Two. His report was so unique that, as far as I know, there have been no other published articles replicating this experience. Try finding on the internet articles about Lazarus's second death and burial. You will see what I mean. We read in the New Testament about Jesus raising Lazarus from the dead in the small town of Bethany near Jerusalem in about 33 AD. It is a spectacular, mind-boggling miracle performed by Jesus!

All of Jesus miracles were thrilling, but this one was earth shattering. Lazarus had been in his tomb for four days when Jesus arrived on the scene to call him to rise from the dead. Even Lazarus's sister, Martha, was afraid his body would have decayed after this period of time and would produce quite a stench. She tried to caution Jesus about his intentions. Yet when Jesus says, "Lazarus, come out!" Lazarus leaves his tomb and reveals that he is now completely alive. We are captivated when we read about this event in the Bible. Still, we would love to know about the life of Lazarus after he defeats death at the hands of our Savior. Fred Overton had an idea about that.

Fred stated that, in the summer of 1945, he had visited the site of Lazarus' second burial. He believed he had received confirmation that it was the same Lazarus who was raised from the dead by Jesus. What caused him to be so sure?

After returning from Germany, his unit was stationed on the outskirts of Marseilles, France. They were waiting for a troop transport to take them to China for the planned invasion of Japan. While on a pass one afternoon, he met up with a guide who was leading a group through the catacombs of one of the adjacent mountains. During the trip through the passageways inside the mountain, the group stopped in a large room with a tomb that was inscribed Lazarus 44 AD. Was this the Lazarus that Jesus raised from the dead?

The guide tells a very convincing story about the apostle Paul and Lazarus being together. For the previous nineteen centuries people in southern France had been taught that Paul, who in the New Testament expressed his hope to visit Spain, actually did make the trip with Lazarus being one of his helpers. This was ten to twelve years after Jesus brought Lazarus forth from the grave near Bethany.

Local history says that Paul's group was shipwrecked near Marseilles. They then hid from the criminal element in the catacombs, and Lazarus unfortunately experienced his second physical death and was entombed there. Fred believed from the accounting given to him that Paul started his journey to Spain, even though it was not recorded in the Bible, and that Lazarus was with him when he died a second death.

Fred had hoped to one day read about this story in a newspaper or magazine, and even meet someone else in the States who had visited Lazarus' tomb. However, for over half a century, there was nothing. Then on a trip from his home in Indiana to Michigan he met a man who had served in the Navy during World War Two. He had been docked near Marseilles and the officer in charge of his ship had ordered all his crew to visit the tomb. So, finally, Fred met someone who had shared the same experience as he!

Fred was an avid historian and loved recounting his story

about Lazarus and many others. He wrote many articles about different experiences he had in life and had several published in the *Odon Journal* in Odon, Indiana. I wished I could have personally met him to talk about his exciting life.

Fred died in 2016 at the age of 93. He is now with the Lord, and I am sure he has the answers to many of his questions, including those he had about the true follow-up story of Lazarus. He now has verification about the memory stones he found in France after World War Two. Perhaps Lazarus himself has shared all of that with him.

Whatever the truth is about Lazarus, I believe his story continued in the years after his life was extended and then on into eternity. I saw a television show recently called "Forever Young" which highlights very talented senior citizens who are still using the talents the Lord has given them. Many of them are in their seventies, eighties, and even nineties. They are still singing, dancing, performing comedy routines and demonstrating acrobatic acts. Watching these inspirational people perform, I just can't believe their talents cease to exist when their mortal bodies quit functioning. Surely, if they believe in our Lord, they will continue to delight and bless others when they continue their eternal journey into heaven. Perhaps, their gifts just become even more spectacular after our Father has lifted their earthly burdens from their spirits!

I think the rest of *our* story is like Fred's journey to find more evidence about Lazarus. God wants us to hunger for more. He wants us to hunger for *Him*. That is why He placed a yearning for eternity in our souls. God's memory stones surely continue being gifts to us after we are home with restored bodies. I wonder if God will point out to us the ones we failed to notice during our earthly lives. How many did he give us, but we were just too busy and distracted to notice? Maybe He will tell us, "Don't worry. I am giving you many, many more as we spend eternity together." I am sure we will savor every one of those! Thank you Father! You are unparalleled in the universe!

I have a white robe hanging on the door of the closet in my prayer room. Every time I enter that closet to crowd in more "stuff," I remember my ultimate goal for wearing attire is to have my Lord dress me in a white robe of righteousness. None of the things that clutter this closet will matter then. None of the worries and cares that clutter my spirit today will matter then.

I joyfully anticipate joining loved ones who have gone ahead, and hearing their stories about the memory stones they have experienced with our Lord in the heavenly realm. Someday I will finish my time here on earth, and then when their life stories are complete, my children and grandchildren will follow me into the arms of Jesus. I will have memory stones to share with them that He has given me while I awaited their arrival. That is going to be spectacular!

The Cornelius Family

May all generations of our family and yours someday have a
reunion in heaven as we celebrate being with the living God and
bask in His light!

Isaiah 59: 20-21

"The Redeemer will come to Zion, and to those who turn from transgression in Jacob," says the LORD. "As for me," says the LORD, "this is My covenant with them: My Spirit who is upon you, and My words which I have put in your mouth, shall not depart from your mouth, nor from the mouth of your descendants, nor from the mouth of your descendants' descendants," says the LORD, "from this time and forevermore."

169

My mother-in-law, Vera Cardinal Cornelius
1922-2008

Resides in heaven with our Lord

My mother, Martha Overstreet Spencer
1919-2014

Resides in heaven with our Lord

Epilogue

I have been blessed in so many ways while writing this book. For two years, I had just the title and the rough draft of two chapters. Finally, a few months ago, I heard the Lord say to me very clearly in my spirit, "If you will just sit in front of your computer and type, I will give you the book. I have it, and I am going to give it to you."

When I was obedient to His message, the book came quickly. So much so, I could barely type the words fast enough. That is how the Holy Spirit works in us! I called a friend, who had been praying for me and the completion of this book, to give her an update. She told me, "I have been praying every day for your book for two years!" God knows us so well, and He will always put people in place to support us when He has an assignment for us. He always gives us the resources and faith to complete what He has placed in hearts to do for His kingdom.

The times I wavered with what I felt I had been called to do, He sent encouragement from others and unique, joyful circumstances to strengthen my resolve. Recently, one of my friends gave me an envelope of wood shavings from a campground meeting she had attended. The new shavings had a fresh, clean woodsy smell. The message from these shavings was that we are new in Christ every day, and we need to celebrate each day fully! Think about the fragrance of us experiencing this with our Lord! Wouldn't it be wonderful to leave this fragrance everywhere we go?

Every day the Lord is speaking to us and asking us to pay attention to the blessings He is placing in our lives. Some days we have laughter and joy and other days we have mostly stress and sorrow. Whatever we are experiencing, our Lord is giving us Himself to carry us through. He is asking us to remember what He did in our lives yesterday, carry that remembrance with us today, and rejoice in our faith about the future with Him. There is so much celebration yet to come with our living God. More than we can ever, ever comprehend! Praise Him! Tell others the good news!

Jesus is speaking to us every day. Listen for Him.

Bob Mulford

About the Author

Barbara Cornelius grew up in a small town in Indiana, and like her father and three of her grandparents, became a teacher. She enjoyed teaching math and science for over thirty years. In retirement, she has found great joy in writing true stories about the living God as she sees Him in her everyday life and in the lives of others who have been touched by Him.

She has been married to the love of her life, Larry Cornelius, for fifty-one years and has been blessed with a daughter and son. A wonderful son-in-law and daughter-in-law also came into her life as children of her heart. True prosperity continued for her with the birth of each of her eight grandchildren. God has drenched her in blessings!

Her first book, Lazarus Still Rises is about miracles she has seen in her own life and how God is still giving them to the world, just like the ones described in the Bible. Her second book, God's Postmarks, recounts signs that the Lord is providing every day to reveal how He is still at work in our lives. This third book, God's Memory Stones, is about the personal memories of love God gives us.

It is her fervent prayer that these books encourage people to see how thrilling and engaged God is with the lives of His people. They will find God when they look for Him and search for knowledge of Him. He is AWESOME!

CPSIA information can be obtained
at www.ICGtesting.com
Printed in the USA
FSOW03n2229271217
42443FS